THE BASKETBALL HALL OF FAME'S

HOOP FACTS AND STATS

Alex Sachare

D1444049

A MOUNTAIN LION BOOK

John Wiley & Sons, Inc.
New York • Chichester • Weinheim • Brisbane • Singapore • Toronto

796.323
S4C

Library of Congress Cataloging-in-Publication Data

ISBN 0-471-19266-X

Printed in the United States of America
10 9 8 7 6 5 4 3 2 1

For Lori.
You mean everything to me.

A.S.

Acknowledgments

Many books were used as source material in the preparation of this manuscript, as well as newspaper and magazine articles and information from various sites on the internet. Among the most valuable books were: *The Official NBA Guide* and *NBA Register*, 1997 editions, published by the *Sporting News*; *The Official NBA Basketball Encyclopedia, Second Edition* by Alex Sachare (with previous editions by Zander Hollander); *The Basketball Hall of Fame's 100 Greatest Basketball Players of All Time* and *100 Greatest Basketball Moments of All Time*, both by Alex Sachare; *The NBA Finals* by Roland Lazenby; *The NBA at 50*, by Mark Vancil; the 1997 editions of the *Official NCAA Men's, Women's* and *Final Four Records*; *Inside Sports Magazine's Complete Guide to College Basketball* by Mike Douchant; the 1997 National High School Sports Record Book, edited by John Gillis; *Sports Illustrated's 1997 Sports Almanac*; *Basketball, It's Origin and Development* by James Naismith; *24 Seconds to Shoot* by Leonard Koppett, *The Complete Book of Basketball, A New York Times Scrapbook History*; *The Night Wilt Scored 100* by Eric Nadel; *Basketball's Great Moments* by Jack Clary; *America's Dream Team* by Chuck Daly with Alex Sachare; *From Set Shot to Slam Dunk* by Charles Salzberg; *Cages to Jump Shots* by Robert W. Peterson; *From Peachbaskets to Slamdunks* by Robert D. Bole and Alfred C. Lawrence; *Vintage NBA* by Neil D. Isaacs; *The History of Professional Basketball* by Glenn Dickey; and *The Encyclopedia of the NCAA Basketball Tournament* by Jim Savage. All are highly recommended to learn more about the sport of basketball.

Special thanks go to Basketball Hall of Fame research specialist Wayne Patterson, Gary K. Johnson of the NCAA and John Gillis of the National Federation of State High School Associations for their assistance in providing source material for use in the preparation of their chapters.

If you happen to be in the area of Springfield, Mass., try to visit the Naismith Memorial Basketball Hall of Fame, which includes videos, multi-media exhibits and interactive activities as well as a wide array of memorabilia in addition to the Honors Court, where the inductees are featured. It is well worth the time.

Photo Credits: Special thanks to Max Crandall, designer and illustrator; Wayne Patterson, photo researcher, Naismith Memorial Basketball Hall of Fame; Joanna Bruno, sales representative, AP Wide World Photos; Ellen Pollak, Library of Congress.

CONTENTS

INTRODUCTION

ROOTS OF THE GAME

Dr. Luther Gulick, head of the physical education department at the YMCA Training School (now Springfield College) in 1891, had a problem.

Winters in Springfield, Massachusetts, as throughout New England, can be long, cold, and snowy. How was he going to keep his students in good physical condition without being able to take them outdoors? He approached a young Canadian-born instructor named Dr. James Naismith and asked him to think up an indoor activity that would provide an "athletic distraction" for his students. Gulick wanted something that would keep the students interested and help them burn energy.

Naismith thought about taking popular outdoor games like soccer and lacrosse and bringing them indoors, but he decided these would be too physical for indoors. He needed something active but not quite as violent. Faced with a similar challenge during his student days at McGill University in Montreal, Naismith had helped the school's rugby players stay in shape by having them run and flip a ball into a box on the gymnasium floor. He also remembered an outdoor game from his childhood called Duck on a Rock in which players tossed small stones at a larger stone set up as a target. Both activities stressed the hand-eye coordination so valuable in all sports, but the players didn't have the physical contact that marked the outdoor sports. By combining them, Naismith came up with the idea of a game in which teams of players would move about the gymnasium floor to try to get into position to shoot a ball into a raised target—Naismith stressed that the target must be high so as to promote skill, agility, and finesse rather than brute force.

Naismith drew up an original set of 13 rules for his new activity and set about getting the gymnasium ready for it. Getting balls was easy—soccer balls were readily available. However, the targets presented a problem. Naismith asked custodian Pop Stebbins to find a pair of boxes and nail them to the wooden running track that circled the gymnasium, 10 feet above the floor. But Stebbins couldn't find any boxes that were the right size and instead returned to the gymnasium with a couple of round peach baskets. Naismith gave him the okay, and thus the game became known as "basket ball" rather than "box ball" (and "hoops" rather than "squares"). Naismith's students wanted the game to be called "Naismith ball," but the modest teacher wouldn't hear of it.

THE VERY FIRST GAME

There were 18 boys in Naismith's class, so the first game ever played on December 21, 1891, had nine players on each team, competing in a gym that measured just 50 feet by 35 feet. The teams played two 15-minute halves and only one goal was made—a 25-foot toss by William R. Chase that made the final score of the first basketball game 1-0.

By combining a rugby conditioning drill and a childhood game called Duck on a Rock, **Dr. James Naismith** created the game of basketball.

When Naismith's students went home for the winter holidays, they took word of this new indoor game they had played to the gyms and youth centers in their hometowns. Thus, the game quickly spread up and down the East Coast and as far west as Chicago. Within a year it was being played throughout the United States, and since five of Naismith's original students were from Canada and one was from Japan, it began to take root worldwide.

A 2-2 TIE

Women soon began playing basketball in 1893. Senda Berenson Abbott, a gym teacher at Smith College, promoted the game and became known as the "Mother of Women's Basketball."

Barely two months after Naismith introduced basketball to his students at the YMCA Training School, the first competitive game between teams from different organizations was played. Two branches of the Springfield, Massachusetts, YMCA—the Central YMCA and the Armory Hill YMCA—played to a 2-2 tie on February 12, 1892. One month later the Springfield YMCA Training School's students beat the school's faculty 5-1 in a game that attracted some 200 fans.

Meanwhile, Senda Berenson Abbott, director of physical education at Smith College in Northampton, Massachusetts, read about basketball in a magazine and figured that if it worked for young men, why wouldn't it work for young women? She met with Naismith to learn more about the game and decided she could use it in her classes at Smith, which is where the first women's game on record was played on March 22, 1893. No men were allowed to attend. Abbott continued to promote the game and wrote the first basketball guide for women. Just as Naismith is regarded as the "Father of Basketball," Abbott is widely considered the "Mother of Women's Basketball."

ENTERING THE COLLEGE RANKS

Basketball, introduced to YMCA members, quickly became popular at colleges. In 1892, the game was played by students at Yale, Stanford, Geneva, and Pennsylvania College. The first college team to play basketball against an outside opponent was the University of Toronto, which beat the Toronto YMCA 2-1 in a game played in January, 1893—barely more than a year after Naismith had invented the game. One month later, Vanderbilt University defeated the Nashville, Tennessee, YMCA 9-6 in the first recorded game between an American college team and an outside opponent. The first intercollegiate games on record took place in 1895, when Minnesota A&M beat Hamline 9-3 and Haverford beat Temple 6-4.

College basketball rapidly grew in popularity—the game was a perfect outlet for school spirit and pride. For many years colleges only played other schools in their immediate areas, but in the 1920s and 1930s teams began playing schools from other parts of the country. These games spurred the sport's growth by allowing many people to see the great players and coaches whose fame used to be limited to the schools' conferences.

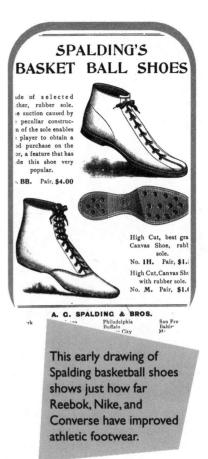

SPALDING'S BASKET BALL SHOES

ide of selected ther, rubber sole, e suction caused by peculiar construc- n of the sole enables player to obtain a od purchase on the or, a feature that has de this shoe very popular.

. BB.   Pair, $4.00

High Cut, best gra Canvas Shoe, rubt sole.
No. 1H.   Pair, $1.
High Cut, Canvas Sh with rubber sole.
No. M.   Pair, $1.

A. G. SPALDING & BROS.

rk   Philadelphia   San Fra
             Buffalo   Baltir
             City   M

This early drawing of Spalding basketball shoes shows just how far Reebok, Nike, and Converse have improved athletic footwear.

MARCH MADNESS IN 1938?

The first truly national collegiate championship was held in 1938, when the Metropolitan Basketball Writers Association of New York organized the National Invitation Tournament (NIT). They invited six teams from various parts of the country to compete at Madison Square Garden, along with host schools New York University and Long Island University. Temple beat Colorado 60-36 for the championship of the first NIT, which proved so popular that the writers turned to the local coaches' organization to run the tournament after that.

But many members of the National Association of Basketball Coaches (NABC), especially in the Midwest, didn't like the idea of a national champion being determined in an Eastern tournament created by New York sportswriters. So, in 1939, they created their own tournament, inviting eight teams to compete at Northwestern University in Evanston, Illinois. Oregon beat Ohio

State 46-33 for the title, but attendance was low and the tournament lost money. The NABC was forced to ask the NCAA to step in and take it over.

The NIT remained the big college tournament through World War II. In 1944, for example, Utah chose to participate in the NIT over the NCAA. But after losing in the first round of the NIT, the Utes accepted a late bid to join the NCAA field after all—and went on to win the title. It wasn't until 1947, when Holy Cross became the first Eastern school to win the NCAA crown, that the NCAA tournament started to catch up to the NIT in prestige. The NCAA overtook the NIT during the 1950s and 1960s, then rode the college basketball boom to become one of the major sports events in the 1980s and 1990s. The NIT continues but as a lesser tournament for teams that do not qualify for the NCAA event.

The match-up between Indiana State forward **Larry Bird** and Michigan State guard **Magic Johnson** in the 1979 NCAA championship became known as the game that changed college basketball.

PLAYING FOR MONEY

The first professional game that can be documented took place in Trenton, New Jersey, in 1896, although there are reports of a pro game being played in Herkimer, New York, three years earlier. A group of basketball players in Trenton, who regularly played at a local YMCA, found that facility unavailable one day. They decided to rent a local Masonic Hall and charge admission to help pay the expenses. Any profits would be split among the players. Many spectators showed up and the game was a success, with each player earning $15 after expenses were covered. There was $1 left over and that went to Fred Cooper, the Trenton team captain who had organized the game and even designed the team uniforms, which included velvet shorts and tights. Cooper thus became the first highest paid player in basketball history.

THE NBL

The first known professional league was formed in 1898 and was called the National Basketball League, but since all teams came from the Philadelphia area, it was far from national. Over the next half-century there would be many leagues, although the most successful professional teams made most of their money by barnstorming—traveling from one city to another, playing one-night stands against local opponents wherever they went. Teams like the Buffalo Germans, the Troy Trojans, the Original Celtics, the Rens, the SPHAs and the Harlem Globetrotters often bypassed league play entirely, choosing to hit the road in order to survive.

One of the strongest of the early leagues was the American Basketball League that existed from 1925 to 1931, but the Depression put an end to it. The next significant league, which also took the name of the National Basketball League, was formed in 1937. Backed by large companies like General Electric, Goodyear, and Firestone, the National Basketball League (NBL) was based in the Midwest and lasted a dozen years. But although it achieved a high level of play, its future was limited by the small towns and arenas in which it played.

PERFECT TIMING

With the end of World War II in 1945, a new era in American professional sports was beginning. Among the team sports, baseball was booming, football was starting to grow, and hockey held its regional appeal, but basketball had yet to catch on, at least not professionally. But with so many soldiers coming home, all of a sudden people had both money and

The 1992 Olympic Dream Team was labeled as the greatest basketball team ever assembled in the history of the sport.

leisure time and were looking for more entertainment. Looking back, the birth of a major professional basketball league seems inevitable.

On June 6, 1946, the owners of the major arenas and hockey teams from Boston, Chicago, Cleveland, Detroit, New York, Philadelphia, Pittsburgh, Providence, St. Louis, Toronto, and Washington, D.C., met at the old Commodore Hotel alongside New York's Grand Central Terminal. They came with one purpose—to find another event to draw people on nights when their arenas would otherwise sit idle. They already had hockey, the circus, and ice shows, so they turned to basketball, which already was tremendously popular on the college and scholas-tic levels. After the meeting, they announced the formation of the Basketball Association of America (BAA) to begin play that fall.

On November 1, 1946, the New York Knicks beat the Toronto Huskies 68-66 at Toronto's Maple Leaf Gardens in the new league's first game. Toronto player-coach Ed Sadowski was the high scorer with 18 points, but it was New York's Ossie Schectman who scored the game's first basket. Tickets were priced from $2.50 to 75 cents, and the league was promotion-minded even then—any fan taller than 6' 8" Toronto center George Nostrance was admitted free.

BIG CITIES, BIG MONEY

The birth of the BAA signaled the end for the NBL, which could not compete against the new league's larger cities and arenas. In 1948, the BAA added four of the strongest teams from the NBL, including the defending champion Minneapolis Lakers, who featured the sport's greatest player, George Mikan. One year later the NBL folded, with six survivors merging into the BAA. The resulting league was renamed the National Basketball Association (NBA), with BAA head Maurice Podoloff serving as its first president.

The NBA struggled to gain acceptance for many years, and from 1967 through 1976 it had to compete for talent and fans with the upstart American Basketball Association (ABA). But the ABA was never in strong financial shape and finally folded, with four survivors joining an NBA that now numbered 22 teams. That paved the way for a new era of stability, growth, and prosperity for the NBA in the 1980s and 1990s, marked by the arrival of popular stars like Magic Johnson, Larry Bird, and Michael Jordan and the leadership of marketing-minded commissioner David Stern. Today fans all around the world know the 29-team NBA and its stars.

While basketball was grow-ing in the United States, it was growing around the world as well. In 1936, men's basketball was added to the Olympic Games as an official medal sport. Fittingly, the man who started it all, Dr. James Naismith, was brought to the Olympics in Berlin to see the inaugural event.

Basketball's world popularity increased dramatically with the creation of the Dream Team for the 1992 Olympic Games in Barcelona. The longtime ban against NBA players competing in the Olympics was lifted. Finally the greatest sports event in the world was open to the best basketball players in the world, just as it is open to the best athletes in other sports. The Dream Team captured the imagination of fans not just in Barcelona but throughout Europe and the world, who delighted in seeing—many for the first time—the beautiful sport of basketball played to such a high level by stars like Jordan, Johnson, Bird, and the rest.

BY THE RULES

The rules of basketball have been changing almost constantly ever since the ink dried on James Naismith's original 13 rules. Hardly a year goes by when some governing body doesn't make a significant rules change affecting one level of the sport or another—high school, college, professional, international, men, or women.

Although there has been significant effort to try to reduce or eliminate the differences in recent years, there will never be one set of rules for all levels of basketball. Nor should there be. It makes no sense to have high school girls playing by the same rules as professional men.

They don't even use the same ball. The basketball used at all levels of the women's game, from high school to the pros, is roughly an inch smaller in size and just a bit lighter in weight than the ball used by their male counterparts.

There even are differences in court size. While the pros and collegians use a court that is standardized at 50 feet wide by 94 feet long, the National Federation of State High School Associations says high school boys and girls may compete on a court that is 10 feet shorter, although many play on 94-foot courts for convenience.

Perhaps no rules change in the modern era helped the development of the sport of basketball more than the invention of the shot clock by Danny Biasone, owner of the NBA's Syracuse Nationals, in 1954. Until that time a team could take as long as it wanted before shooting the ball, and this led to many instances of stalling. The NBA, not even 10 years old and struggling to draw fans, needed something to speed up its game so it adapted the shot clock, which forced a team to attempt a shot within 24 seconds or else lose possession of the ball. Similar shot clocks have been instituted in the college ranks and in international ball, although the time limits have fluctuated over the years. The NBA, by contrast, has always kept it at 24 seconds.

Dr. James Naismith's Original 13 Rules

The object of the game is to put the ball into your opponent's goal. This may be done by throwing the ball from any part of the grounds, with one or both hands, under the following conditions and rules.

The ball to be an ordinary association football (soccer ball).

1. The ball may be thrown in any direction with one or both hands.

2. The ball may be batted in any direction with one or both hands (never with a fist).

3. A player cannot run with the ball. The player must throw it from the spot on which he catches it, allowance to be made for a man who catches the ball when running if he tries to stop.

4. The ball must be held by the hands. The arms or body must not be used for holding it.

5. No shouldering, holding, pushing, tripping, or striking in any way the person of an opponent shall be allowed; the first infringement of this rule by any player shall count as a foul, the second shall disqualify him until the next goal is made, or, if there was evident intent to injure the person, for the whole of the game, no substitute allowed.

6. A foul is striking at the ball with the fist, violation of Rules 3, 4, and such as described in Rule 5.

7. If either side makes three consecutive fouls it shall count as a goal for the opponents (consecutive means without the opponents in the meantime making a foul).

8. A goal shall be made when the ball is thrown or batted from the grounds into the basket and stays there, providing those defending the goal do not touch or disturb the goal. If the ball rests on the edges, and the opponent moves the basket, it shall count as a goal.

9. When the ball goes out of bounds, it shall be thrown into the field of play by the person first touching it. He has a right to hold it unmolested for five seconds. In case of a dispute the umpire shall throw it straight into the field. The thrower-in is allowed five seconds; if he holds it longer it shall go to the opponent. If any side persists in delaying the game the umpire shall call a foul on that side.

10. The umpire shall be the judge of the men and shall note the fouls and notify the referee when three consecutive fouls have been made. He shall have power to disqualify men according to Rule 5.

11. The referee shall be judge of the ball and shall decide when the ball is in play, in bounds, to which side it belongs, and shall keep the time. He shall decide when a goal has been made and keep account of the goals, with any other duties that are usually performed by a referee.

12. The time shall be two fifteen minute halves, with five minutes rest between.

13. The side making the most goals in that time shall be declared the winner. In the case of a draw the game may, by agreement of the captains, be continued until another goal is made.

A GLOBAL GAME INTO THE 21ST CENTURY

Basketball is booming, growing by leaps and bounds—or is that rebounds?

The steady thump-thump-thump of a basketball being dribbled may be heard from the asphalt schoolyards of Harlem in New York to the dirt driveways of Indiana farm country to the beachside courts in California. Basketball is played in more high schools, by girls as well as boys, than any other sport in the United States. Michael Jordan is the best-known athlete in the world. And at high schools throughout the country, basketball is the sport that raises school spirit and draws students together through the long winter months.

NBA players are household names, true heroes to a generation of young fans who know them as Michael or Shaq, Sir Charles or Scottie, Penny or Grant, the Mailman or the Dream. They're not just in the sports section of the local newspaper but on the movie, music and fashion pages as well, and youngsters take notice. When fifth grade students at a school in New Jersey were asked if any of them could name 10 major league baseball players, none could do it. But when asked to name 10 NBA players, 17 out of 18 raised their hands, and before long the list had grown to 35 names.

Michael Jordan is not merely a basketball player. He is an icon, a hero—who better to star in a movie opposite cartoon legend Bugs Bunny?

Basketball's popularity knows no national boundary. It is the fastest growing sport in the world, competing with soccer (or football, as it is known everywhere but in the United States) for the top spot. It's growing especially fast among younger fans. Boys and girls from Barcelona to Beijing and beyond are just as likely to be seen dribbling a basketball with their hands as kicking a soccer ball with their feet.

When NBA officials traveled to Spain, in October, for the 1988 McDonald's Open, a worldwide tournament that featured the Boston Celtics that year, they were greeted by something many thought they'd never see. When they arrived for a nine o'clock meeting at the offices of Real Madrid, the city's top sports club, they saw a long line of fans around the giant outdoor stadium. Were they lining up to buy tickets to a big soccer match? No, they had been there since six o'clock in the morning for the chance to buy tickets to see Larry Bird and the legendary Celtics. "Football is our fathers' sport," one youngster who looked to be about 14 years old explained. "Basketball is our sport."

David Stern, the NBA commissioner, frequently talks of visiting China with his wife and being amazed by the number of fans asking him about the Red Oxen. It took him awhile to realize they were referring to the Chicago Bulls, whose logo does indeed resemble a red ox. And when the members of the first Dream Team came together for the Barcelona Olympics, they captured the imagination of the world's youth and were mobbed by fans and fellow athletes wherever they went. Coach Chuck Daly compared it to "traveling with a dozen rock stars."

This tremendous growth in popularity did not just happen. As foreign governments changed, American culture was allowed to spread. For basketball, the timing of this new wave of freedom couldn't have been better. Larry Bird and Magic Johnson won millions of new fans for the sport with their brilliant play and passion for the game. Then Michael Jordan came along and, with his sensational style, took it all to another level. NBA games are seen on television in more than 180 countries around the world. NBA caps, t-shirts and other merchandise can be found wherever you go, from Toronto to Tel Aviv to Tokyo.

Kids love basketball. It's a fundamentally simple sport— virtually any number can play, and the only equipment really needed is a hoop and a ball. The basic premise is a simple one: whichever team puts the ball through the hoop more often wins. Yet something about the game makes fans stay fans for life. Basketball is a game of five talents playing with one ball, and success comes only when all six of those things work together. Parents love the lessons basketball can teach; teamwork, sacrifice, yet still aggressiveness. The lessons learned on the court can serve well throughout life.

Like all sports, part of what adds to the mystique of basketball is its history. Why is a basket 10 feet high, and has it always been that way? Did Wilt Chamberlain really score 100 points in an NBA game? And who is Lisa Leslie, who once scored 101 points in one half of a high school game? These questions and many, many more are answered in *The Basketball Hall of Fame's Hoop Facts & Stats*.

This book introduces young fans to the great sport of basketball, its rich past, glorious present and promising future. *Hoop Facts & Stats* includes stories and biographies and deals with the fascinating numbers that add up to the sport of basketball. Readers of all ages can understand and appreciate these stats, and the clear language and layout of the book. This is both a serious book, presented by the Naismith Memorial Basketball Hall of Fame, and a fun book, because for young and old alike, sports should be fun.

To learn more about basketball, we recommend you visit your local library or bookstore. If you are lucky enough to have the chance to, visit the Naismith Memorial Basketball Hall of Fame in Springfield, Massachusetts, you should go. It's truly a living shrine to the sport, with video and audio tapes, interactive games and activities and exciting exhibits that bring the sport's history to life. it honors great athletes, teams, and accomplishments from all levels of the sport. Most of all, get involved—and not just by watching games on TV or at your local school, playground or arena. Find a hoop, pick up a basketball, get the feel of it against your palms and fingers, then dribble it a few times before you take your best shot. Chances are your first shot will miss, but don't get discouraged. Michael Jordan was cut from his high school team the first time he tried out, and look at him now!

TEN RECORDS THAT MAY NEVER BE BROKEN

Michael Jordan is arguably the best basketball player to ever play the game.

But do you think he'll ever score 100 points in a game as Wilt Chamberlain did in 1962? Indiana University's Bobby Knight once coached his team to a perfect season in 1976, winning all 32 games they played. But can you ever imagine him leading his Hoosiers to win 88 games in a row as UCLA accomplished under coach John Wooden?

Basketball is growing at all levels as never before. Yet is has been around for more than 100 years and has had enough time to produce its share of records that seem likely to last forever. Some records are relatively new, while others already have withstood the test of time and are likely to remain the record books for many years to come. Here's a top 10 list of records that are likely to be with us for a while.

1. **Wilt Chamberlain Scores 100 Points in an NBA Game**
   On March 2, 1962, Wilt Chamberlain scorched the New York Knicks for 100 points, leading his Philadelphia Warriors to a 169-147 victory. It's the most points ever scored in an NBA game and is 22 points more than the next highest mark, which was Chamberlain's 78 points against Los Angeles earlier that same season.

   Why It Will Last
   Basketball players in general are taller, stronger, faster and better jumpers now than ever before. That means the com-

petition is greater, night in and night out. The best players are less likely to come up against a "soft touch," even on the worst teams. Today's "ordinary" NBA players possess physical skills that would dazzle the players who came before them.

Another factor is the increase in team defense throughout the NBA. If Chamberlain were playing today, he would find himself guarded by two or three players every time he touched the ball in the low post (near the basket). This "doubling down," as it's called by coaches, makes it unlikely any center will ever challenge the century mark. And the chances of a smaller player being able to drive or jump-shoot his way to 100 points seem very slim indeed.

2. Harvey Catchings, Eric Money, Ralph Simpson, and Al Skinner Played for Both New Jersey and Philadelphia in the Same NBA Game

On November 8, 1978, the Philadelphia 76ers beat the New Jersey Nets 137-133. But the Nets filed a protest, claiming referee Richie Powers had improperly called a third technical foul against New Jersey coach Kevin Loughery and player Bernard King. Since players and coaches are supposed to be ejected from the game after two technicals, Commissioner Larry O'Brien upheld the protest and ordered the game replayed from the time the calls were made.

The teams scheduled the replay for March 23, 1979, before a regularly scheduled game between the two clubs. But on February 7, New Jersey had traded Money and Skinner to Philadelphia for Catchings, Simpson, and cash. Thus, when the game was continued, the four players competed for the opposite team from which they had started the game. None of the players had much of an effect on the outcome. Philadelphia, leading 84-81 when play resumed, won the replay 123-117.

"I remember looking at the box score the next day and seeing my name for both Philadelphia and New Jersey. It was kind of weird, to say the least," said Catchings.

Why It Will Last

Playing for both teams in the same game is a record that at most can only be tied but never broken. It's highly unlikely that even that will happen, since replays are extremely rare. The commissioner will only order a replay if there was a clear problem with a rule, which hardly ever happens. And what are the chances of the two teams involved in a protested game working out a trade? The only other way a player could play for both teams in the same game would be if he was traded during the first half, switched uniforms at half-time and suited up for the other team in the second half, which has never happened.

3. ULCA Wins 88 Games in a Row

The ULCA Bruins, coached by Hall of Fame John Wooden and featuring Bill Walton as their center, won 88 consecutive games from 1971 to 1974, when their streak was ended by Notre Dame. It is by far the longest streak in men's NCAA Division I play, with San Francisco's 60 wins from 1955 to 1957 standing second.

Why It Will Last

There are more good teams in college basketball these days, and they play each other more often. There are nationally televised games between top 20 teams every weekend. There's more travel, which is hard on teams, with major pre-season and mid-season tournaments being held in places like Alaska and Hawaii. These factors make it much harder for a team to put together even one unbeaten season.

Bill Walton was the big man in the paint for UCLA during their incredible 88-game winning streak. Walton was dominant under the glass for the Bruins, guiding them to one of the most extraordinary records in sports.

Wilt Chamberlain was best known for his scoring, but his game was never one-dimensional. He could dribble, pass, and rebound with the best of them.

But perhaps the biggest factor weighing against a college dynasty like UCLA's is that fewer college stars are staying in school for their full four years. With huge amounts of money to be made in the NBA, more and more college standouts are turning pro after just one or two seasons. The star player who stays in school for his full four years is no longer the rule but has become the rare exception.

4. Wilt Chamberlain Grabs 2,149 Rebounds in One NBA Season

Chamberlain, who also holds the NBA single-game (55) and career (23,924) rebounding records, grabbed 2,149 rebounds in the 1960–61 season, his second in the NBA. He also crossed the 2,000 mark the following season. Since 1973, however, only once has an NBA player reached even 1,500 rebounds in any season when Dennis Rodman grabbed 1,530 for Detroit in 1991–92.

Why It Will Last
There are far fewer rebounds in an NBA game today than when Chamberlain set his record because teams are attempting fewer shots per game and mak-ing more of what they attempt. In 1960–61, teams averaged over 73 rebounds per game. Last year that figure was down below 42. Team scoring is down from 118 points per

game to 101, teams average only 81 shots per game instead of 109, and they shoot 46.6 percent instead of 41.5 percent. These trends are not likely to change much, and the combination of fewer shots and better shooting accuracy is a deadly one for anyone seeking to break a rebounding record.

5. The Longest High School Winning Streaks: 159 for Boys, 218 for Girls

The Passaic, New Jersey, high school boys team, known as the "Passaic Wonder Team," won 159 consecutive games from 1919 through 1925, while the Baskin, Louisiana, high school girls team won 218 games in a row from 1947 through 1953. Those stand as the longest winning streaks in high school basketball history.

Why They Will Last

Both streaks are amazing considering that high school players are so young and may not have reached the peak of their skills. There is also so much going on and so many new experiences in high school that it is too much to expect players that age to have the narrowminded focus on winning that the best professional athletes have. Thus, it is quite an accomplishment for a high school team to go through an entire season undefeated—but to put together five or six undefeated seasons is hard to imagine. Also, unlike the NBA, where a player like Karl Malone or Patrick Ewing can star for 10 or 15 years for the same team, a high school player can compete for his school for just three or four years before he moves on. So no one superstar can enable his team to threaten either the boys' or girls' streaks by himself (or herself).

6. Oscar Robertson Averages a Triple-Double for an Entire Season

Long before Magic Johnson brought the phrase "triple-double" into the basketball dictionary, Oscar Robertson was regularly getting double figures in each of three statistical categories in the same game: shooting, re-bounding, and assists. In fact, in the 1961–62 NBA season, the Big O (as the 6' 5", 220-pound Robertson was called) averaged a triple-double for the entire year. Robertson averaged 30.8 points, 12.5 rebounds, and a league-leading 11.4 assists per game in a season that has never been matched. In fact, for his first five NBA seasons, from 1960–61 through

When a player registers a triple-double in a game, it's considered an outstanding achievement. But Hall of Famer **Oscar Robertson** *averaged* a triple-double throughout the entire 1961–62 season.

1964–65, Robertson averaged 30.3 points, 10.4 rebounds, and 10.6 assists per game for the Cincinnati Royals.

Why It Will Last

Today it is considered quite an achievement if a player can post 10 or 12 triple-doubles over the course of an NBA season. There are a number of versatile players—Grant Hill, Scottie Pippen, Penny Hardaway, and Jason Kidd come to mind, along with Michael Jordan, of course—but none is likely to ever approach triple-double figures for an entire season. It's too much to ask a player to score, run a team's offense, and also crash the boards enough to achieve double figures in scoring, assists, and rebounds night in and night out. The 82-game NBA schedule is too demanding. Also, players today tend to be specialists—look at Dennis Rodman, who almost always reaches double figures in rebound-ing but rarely in any other category. Top assists men like John Stockton, Mark Jackson, Rod Strickland, or Damon Stoudamire are not likely to get 10 rebounds, while bangers like Rodman and Karl Malone or centers like Dikembe Mutombo and Shaquille O'Neal can't be expected to dish for 10 assists. And if a player is expected to carry a team's scoring load, you can't ask him to lead the way in assists and rebounds as well.

7. Pete Maravich Scores More Than 48 Percent of LSU's Points in His Career

"Pistol Pete" Maravich holds many major college scoring records, including 28 games of 50 points or more, single-season records of 1,381 points and a 44.5 average, and career records of 3,667 points and a 44.2 average. It's difficult to say which is most likely to stand, but one that appears safe is Maravich's mark of having accounted for 48.19 percent of Louisiana State's points during his college career.

Why It Will Last

There has never been a one-man team like Maravich, and there likely never will be again. The 6' 5" guard accounted for nearly one half of all points scored by his college team in his three varsity seasons. His 48.19 percentage far outdistances his nearest rivals—Wilt Chamberlain of Kansas, 41.04 percent; Bill Bradley of Princeton, 39.60 percent; Oscar Robertson of Cincinnati, 39.41 percent; and Calvin Murphy of Niagara, 38.69 percent. Sure, there will be one-man teams in the future, but it's unlikely any player will dominate like Maravich. Defenses today, with double teams, zones, and gimmicks like box-and-one combinations, will never allow one player to control

When **Pete Maravich** played in college at Louisiana State, freshmen were not allowed to participate in varsity games. His record is amazing, but even more miraculous is that he set it in only three seasons.

the scoring like that again. Also, in all likelihood only a guard would have any chance at all at Maravich's mark, since only a guard does not need someone else to set him up. Maravich would take the inbounds pass, move the ball upcourt against any defensive pressure and get his shot off no matter how many players were guarding him. Unlike a center or a forward, he didn't need someone to get him the ball—an important factor in considering how long his record will last.

Wilt Chamberlain
tested time during the 1961–62 season. Once the first jump ball of the game was tossed up, it was a sure bet the 76er center would be out on the floor for the duration of the game.

8. Wilt Chamberlain Averages 48.5 Minutes Per Game in the 1961–62 Season

An NBA game is 48 minutes long, yet Chamberlain averaged 48.5 minutes for an NBA season—overtimes accounting for the extra minutes. Chamberlain went all the way in 79 of 80 games played in 1961–62, including 47 complete games in a row, and played 3,882 of a possible 3,890 minutes, all league records.

Why It Will Last

Chamberlain's strength and endurance are legendary. He is reknowned for being able to score with opponents leaning on his back and hanging on his arms. What's more, he played when players were expected to go out and play every night. An NBA player in the 1960s did not sit out a game with a minor injury for fear of making it worse. He went out and played. Times have changed. Today players sit out if they feel something might be wrong, if only because they do not want to risk ruining their careers. In addition, Chamberlain was able to travel by bus or train from Philadelphia to many of his team's games. Today's NBA calls for frequent coast-to-coast travel which can sap a player's strength. Finally, the philosophy of coaches has changed so that complete games are far less common today. Even the most prominent players, like Michael Jordan, Karl Malone, and Hakeem Olajuwon, usually are given at least a few minutes on the bench in every half. Coaches would rather rest their stars for a few minutes than play them the full 48, in order to keep them fresh.

9. Bill Chambers of William & Mary Grabs 51 Rebounds in One Game

Playing against Virginia on February 14, 1953, Chambers—who would later become a successful coach at William & Mary—grabbed 51 rebounds to set an NCAA record. No player has ever come close, with the next highest total being 43 by Charlie Slack of Marshall against Morris Harvey the following season.

Why It Will Last

As in the NBA, there are far fewer missed shots, and thus far fewer available rebounds, in college basketball games these days. Tim Duncan of Wake Forest led all major college players in 1996–97 by averaging 14.7 rebounds per game. Entire teams rarely get as many as 51 rebounds in a game—remember, that comes out to more than a rebound a minute. The most dominating big men hardly ever get as many as 20 rebounds in one game—forget about 51. And in today's game, no opponent is going to allow one man to dominate the boards that way.

10. Dale Ellis Plays 69 Minutes in an NBA Game

On November 9, 1989, Dale Ellis of the Seattle SuperSonics played 69 minutes in a 155-154 loss to the Milwaukee Bucks in a game that lasted five overtimes. It's the most minutes played in an NBA game by any player in league history, one more than the 68 minutes log-ged by teammate Xavier McDaniel in that same game. Ellis played all but four of a possible 73 minutes in that marathon.

Why It Will Last

Ellis's game is the longest game in NBA history since the 24-second shot clock was created before the 1954–55 season. There has been one other five-overtime game and one six-overtime contest, but those were before the shot clock speeded up play. In the early years, a team that got possession of the ball in overtime often tried to hold it as long as possible, sometimes even for nearly the full five minutes, before attempting to score. As a result, overtime periods were very low scoring, and some even ended at 0-0. With the shot clock forcing teams to shoot, there is more scoring in overtime and as a result, it's less likely that overtime periods will wind up tied. In order for any player to even have a chance of breaking Ellis's record, he would have to play in a game that lasts at least five overtimes, which is less likely to happen. And then he would have to play almost the entire way, which doesn't happen that often in regular games lasting 48 minutes, let alone overtime contests.

Dale Ellis has always been a threat on offense, sinking more than a few long-range jumpers. But as he displayed on November 9, 1989, Ellis could be counted on for his endurance as well.

Home Cooking

The 88-game win streak held by UCLA will likely remain in the record books forever. However, the Kentucky Wildcats recorded a streak that surpassed 88 games, and had their hometown fans smiling for over a decade.

The Kentucky Wildcats hold the NCAA record for the longest home winning streak. On January 4, 1943, when Kentucky beat Fort Knox 64-43, it began a home-court winning streak that lasted 129 games and stretched over 11 years.

The streak continued through Dec. 30, 1953, when Kentucky beat St. Louis 82-65, then came to an end on January 8, 1954, when Georgia Tech edged the Wildcats 59-58.

The home-court winning streak actually lasted longer than Kentucky's home court. The first 84 games were played in Alumni Gym, then the remainder were in Memorial Coliseum.

NBA RECORDS

CHAMPIONSHIPS

The Boston Celtics have won more championships than any other NBA franchise, 16. The Minneapolis/ Los Angeles Lakers are next with a total of 11 titles.

Under the guidance of Red Auerbach, who served first as coach and then as general manager, the Celtics established the NBA's greatest dynasty, winning eight championships in a row from 1958–59 through 1965–66 and a total of 11 in 13 seasons. Keep in mind that the team that wins the NBA Finals is the league champion, not the team with the best regular season record. Here are the results of the NBA Finals, year-by-year.

NBA Finals, Year-by-Year

Season	Winner, Loser, Result, MVP
1946–47	Philadelphia, Chicago, 4-1, began in 1969
1947–48	Baltimore, Philadelphia, 4-2, began in 1969
1948–49	Minneapolis, Washington, 4-2, began in 1969
1949–50	Minneapolis, Syracuse, 4-2, began in 1969
1950–51	Rochester, New York, 4-3, began in 1969
1951–52	Minneapolis, New York, 4-3, began in 1969
1952–53	Minneapolis, New York, 4-1, began in 1969

Season	Winner, Loser, Result, MVP
1953–54	Minneapolis, Syracuse, 4-3, began in 1969
1954–55	Syracuse, Fort Wayne, 4-3, began in 1969
1955–56	Philadelphia, Fort Wayne, 4-1, began in 1969
1956–57	Boston, St. Louis, 4-3, began in 1969
1957–58	St. Louis, Boston, 4-2, began in 1969
1958–59	Boston, Minneapolis, 4-0, began in 1969
1959–60	Boston, St. Louis, 4-3, began in 1969
1960–61	Boston, St. Louis, 4-1, began in 1969
1961–62	Boston, Los Angeles, 4-3, began in 1969
1962–63	Boston, Los Angeles, 4-2, began in 1969
1963–64	Boston, San Francisco, 4-2, began in 1969
1964–65	Boston , Los Angeles, 4-1, began in 1969
1965–66	Boston , Los Angeles, 4-3, began in 1969
1966–67	Philadelphia, San Francisco, 4-2, began in 1969
1967–68	Boston, Los Angeles, 4-2, began in 1969
1968–69	Boston, Los Angeles, 4-3, Jerry West, L.A.
1969–70	New York, Los Angeles, 4-3, Willis Reed, N.Y.
1970–71	Milwaukee, Baltimore, 4-0, Kareem Abdul-Jabbar, Mil.
1971–72	Los Angeles, New York, 4-1, Wilt Chamberlain, L.A.
1972–73	New York, Los Angeles, 4-1, Willis Reed, N.Y.
1973–74	Boston, Milwaukee, 4-3, John Havlicek, Bos.
1974–75	Golden State, Washington, 4-0, Rick Barry, G.S.
1975–76	Boston, Phoenix, 4-2, Jo Jo White, Bos.
1976–77	Portland, Philadelphia, 4-2, Bill Walton, Port.
1977–78	Washington, Seattle, 4-3, Wes Unseld, Wash.
1978–79	Seattle, Washington, 4-1, Dennis Johnson, Sea.
1979–80	Los Angeles, Philadelphia, 4-2, Magic Johnson, L.A.
1980–81	Boston, Houston, 4-2, Cedric Maxwell, Bos.
1981–82	Los Angeles, Philadelphia, 4-2, Magic Johnson, L.A.
1982–83	Philadelphia, Los Angeles, 4-0, Moses Malone, Phil.

NBA Finals, Year-by-Year (continued)

Season	Winner, Loser, Result, MVP
1983–84	Boston , Los Angeles, 4-3, Larry Bird, Bos.
1984–85	L.A. Lakers, Boston, 4-2, Kareem Abdul-Jabbar, L.A.
1985–86	Boston, Houston, 4-2, Larry Bird, Bos.
1986–87	L.A. Lakers, Boston, 4-2, Magic Johnson, L.A.
1987–88	L.A. Lakers, Detroit, 4-3, James Worthy, L.A.
1988–89	Detroit, L.A. Lakers, 4-0, Joe Dumars, Det.
1989–90	Detroit, Portland, 4-1, Isiah Thomas, Det.
1990–91	Chicago, L.A. Lakers, 4-1, Michael Jordan, Chi.
1991–92	Chicago, Portland, 4-2, Michael Jordan, Chi.
1992–93	Chicago, Phoenix, 4-2, Michael Jordan, Chi.
1993–94	Houston, New York, 4-3, Hakeem Olajuwon, Hou.
1994–95	Houston, Orlando, 4-0, Hakeem Olajuwon, Hou.
1995–96	Chicago, Seattle, 4-2, Michael Jordan, Chi.
1996–97	Chicago, Utah, 4-2, Michael Jordan, Chi.

SCORING

The NBA's major scoring records are dominated by two big men: 7' 2" Kareem Abdul-Jabbar, who played 20 seasons before retiring in 1989, and 7' 1" Wilt Chamberlain, who played 14 seasons before retiring in 1973. Between them, they hold nearly all the records for most points and field goals, whether measured by game, season, or career.

Chamberlain and Abdul-Jabbar were both big men, their achievements matching their stature. Between them they won eight NBA team championships, nine individual scoring titles, and 12 rebounding crowns. Abdul-Jabbar enjoyed more of the team success, his teams winning six league titles, while Chamberlain dominated individually like no other, leading the league in scoring seven times and rebounding 11 times. Strikingly different personalities, each left his mark on the game in his own way, as the following list of various NBA scoring records will show.

George Gervin, who was also known as "The Ice Man," scored an amazing 33 points in one quarter for the San Antonio Spurs.

Regular Season

Most Points in a Game: 100 by Wilt Chamberlain, Philadelphia vs. New York at Hershey, Pennsylvania, March 2, 1962.

Most Points in a Half: 59 by Wilt Chamberlain, Philadelphia vs. New York at Hershey, Pennsylvania, March 2, 1962 (second half).

Most Points in a Quarter: 33 by George Gervin, San Antonio at New Orleans, April 9, 1978 (second quarter).

Most Points in a Season: 4,029 by Wilt Chamberlain, Philadelphia, 1961–62.

Most Points Per Game in a Season: 50.4 by Wilt Chamberlain, Philadelphia, 1961–62.

Most Points in a Career: 38,387 by Kareem Abdul-Jabbar, 1969–89.

Most Points Per Game in a Career: 31.7 by Michael Jordan, 1984–97.

Most Consecutive Games with 10 Points or More: 787 by Kareem Abdul-Jabbar, L.A. Lakers, December 4, 1977–December 2, 1987.

Most Field Goals Made in a Game: 36 by Wilt Chamberlain, Philadelphia vs. New York at Hershey, Pennsylvania, March 2, 1962.

Most Field Goals Made with None Missed in a Game: 18 by Wilt Chamberlain, Philadelphia vs. Baltimore at Pittsburgh, February 24, 1967.

Most Field Goals Made in a Season: 1,597 by Wilt Chamberlain, Philadelphia, 1961–62.

Most Field Goals Made in a Career: 15,837 by Kareem Abdul-Jabbar, 1969–89.

Most Field Goals Attempted in a Game: 63 by Wilt Chamberlain, Philadelphia vs. New York at Hershey, Pennsylvania, March 2, 1962.

Most Field Goals Attempted with None Made in a Game: 17 by Tim Hardaway, Golden State at San Antonio, December 27, 1991.

Most Field Goals Attempted in a Season: 3,159 by Wilt Chamberlain, Philadelphia, 1961-62.

Most Field Goals Attempted in a Career: 28,307 by Kareem Abdul-Jabbar, 1969–89.

Highest Field Goal Percentage in a Season: .727 by Wilt Chamberlain, Los Angeles, 1972–73.

Highest Field Goal Percentage in a Career: .599 by Artis Gilmore, 1976–88.

Playoffs

Most Points in a Game: 63 by Michael Jordan, Chicago at Boston, April 20, 1986.

Most Points in a Half: 39 by Eric "Sleepy" Floyd, Golden State vs. L.A. Lakers, May 10, 1987.

Most Points in a Quarter: 29 by Eric "Sleepy" Floyd, Golden State vs. L.A. Lakers, May 10, 1987.

Most Points Per Game in a One Playoff Series: 46.3 by Jerry West, Los Angeles vs. Baltimore, 1965.

Kareem Abdul-Jabbar

His trademark was the sky-hook, a graceful shot taken with a long, sweeping motion of the arm, released from a point so high over his head that it was virtually impossible to block. Kareem Abdul-Jabbar used that sky-hook to score more points than any other player in NBA history (38,387) and earn a place in the Basketball Hall of Fame.

Abdul-Jabbar was born Ferdinand Lewis Alcindor (he changed his name in 1971) and grew up in New York City, where his father worked for the subway system. He first gained national attention as a lean and lanky teenager when he led Power Memorial Academy to a 73-2 record in his years with the varsity.

Recruited by virtually every school in the country because he was a good student as well as a great basketball player, he chose to go to California and play under legendary coach John Wooden at UCLA. In those years freshmen were not permitted to compete on the varsity team, but people on campus were so excited about Abdul-Jabbar that his UCLA freshman team's games drew more fans than the varsity.

Abdul-Jabbar led UCLA to an 88-2 record and three consecutive NCAA championships, becoming the first player to win MVP honors of the Final Four three times. While he was in college, the NCAA officials passed a rule outlawing the dunk shot, supposedly to make scoring more difficult for Abdul-Jabbar and other big men. But talent and dedication will find a way. Abdul-Jabbar seized the opportunity to develop his sky-hook and other shots, and went on to average 26.4 points per game and shoot an NCAA record 63.9 percent.

His success continued into the NBA, where he won Rookie of the Year honors in 1969–70. In his second season, he led the Milwaukee Bucks to the NBA Championship, winning the first of his six MVP awards. After six seasons with Milwaukee, Abdul-Jabbar asked to be traded, either to his original home, New York, or his college home, Los Angeles.

It was a golden opportunity for the Lakers, a chance to get the game's dominant center while in his prime at age 28. So they outbid New York by putting together a package of two starters and two prime rookies and brought Abdul-Jabbar to Los Angeles on June 16, 1975. He stayed for 14 seasons and, when joined in 1980 by Magic Johnson, helped turn the Lakers into the NBA's Team of the Eighties, winning five championships in the decade.

The Los Angeles spotlight was harsh at times, but the attention helped Abdul-Jabbar mature. "For a long time, Kareem shut the door emotionally to a lot of people," reflected Pat Riley, who coached Abdul-Jabbar with the Lakers for nine seasons. "But then he seemed to get more comfortable as he got older, and he opened up a little more."

Abdul-Jabbar showed his fans another aspect of his personality when he starred in the popular 1981 comedy film *Airplane* with Leslie Nielsen. He remains active in the entertainment industry, producing and developing several projects for film and television, many of them dealing with aspects of black history. He recently wrote *Black Profiles in Courage*, a book that describes the contributions made by African-Americans in various fields.

Did you know? Kareem Abdul-Jabbar means "strong and wise soldier" in Arabic.

Wilt Chamberlain

Wilt Chamberlain was a player who was larger than life, in both size and achievement. He stood 7' 1", weighed at least 275 pounds, and was tremendously strong; yet he was quick and agile as well. Chamberlain was unstoppable on offense, once scoring 100 points in a single game for the Philadelphia Warriors against the New York Knicks

Before he entered the NBA, **Wilt Chamberlain** was a star for the original Harlem Globetrotters.

on March 2, 1962, and averaging over 50 points per game for an entire season.

"He is Babe Ruth all over again," said former Warriors owner Eddie Gottlieb, comparing Chamberlain to the great baseball star of the 1920s.

Perhaps a better comparison would have been to Goliath, for Chamberlain dwarfed his opponents. The massive Chamberlain could seemingly score at will, yet he was a gentle giant who never used his might to punish opponents. He avoided fights and did not foul out of a single one of his 1,045 NBA games.

When he was still at Philadelphia's Overbrook High School, Chamberlain was considered ready for the NBA—something that was unheard of back in the 1950s. Instead he went to the University of Kansas for three years, then spent one year with the Harlem Globetrotters.

Once he entered the NBA in 1959, he began rewriting the record book. He scored more points in his rookie season (2,707) than any other player in history. But his best year statistically was 1961–62, when he became the only NBA player to score 4,000 points in a season with 4,029. In that season Chamberlain averaged 50.4 points and 48.5 minutes per game and set the single-

All-Time Leading Scorers

Player	Points
Kareem Abdul-Jabbar	38,387
Wilt Chamberlain	31,419
Moses Malone	27,409
Elvin Hayes	27,313
Michael Jordan	26,920
Oscar Robertson	26,710
Dominique Wilkins	26,534
John Havlicek	26,395
Alex English	25,613
Karl Malone	25,592
Jerry West	25,192
Hakeem Olajuwon	23,650
Robert Parish	23,334
Adrian Dantley	23,177
Charles Barkley	21,756

game scoring record of 100 points against New York.

Chamberlain led the NBA in scoring seven years in a row and was the league's top rebounder in 11 of his 14 seasons. His dominance was such that the league made several major rules changes because of him, widening the foul lane and prohibiting offensive goaltending (knocking a shot away after it has already started its downward arc to the basket).

For all his accomplishments, however, Chamberlain never totally won over his critics. For one thing, he was never a good free throw shooter, making fewer than half his attempts over his career. More importantly, he won only two championships in his 14 NBA seasons, far fewer than his rival, Bill Russell, who won 11 championships in 13 seasons with the Boston Celtics. "It's human nature," Chamberlain said of the criticism. "No one roots for Goliath."

But the criticism bothered him. After winning the scoring title in each of his first seven years, he focused on other aspects of the game as if to prove his talent. He won his first championship with Philadelphia in 1966–67, and the following year he led the league in rebounds, assists, field goal percentage, and minutes played.

Superstar **Michael Jordan** has led the NBA in scoring nine times during his illustrious career.

Chamberlain is quick to point out that Russell almost always had a better group of teammates to support him, and that's why he won more NBA titles. When Chamberlain had strong support, he won, too. His two championship teams, the 1967 Philadelphia Warriors who were 68-13 and the 1972 Los Angeles Lakers who were 69-13, posted the two best marks in NBA history until Michael Jordan led the Chicago Bulls to a 72-10 record in 1995–96.

"He is the greatest basketball player that ever lived. He could do it all," said teammate Tom Gola.

Did you know? In high school and college, Wilt Chamberlain was a track star as well as a basketball standout.

Scoring Champions, Year by Year

Michael Jordan has won nine NBA scoring championships, more than any other player. Wilt Chamberlain is next in line with seven titles. Following is the complete list of NBA scoring champions. Note that from 1946–47 through 1968–69, the scoring champion was the player who scored the most points in that season. Since then it has been the player with the highest scoring average per game, so that a player who misses a few games due to injury or illness still has a chance to win the title.

NBA Scoring Champions

Season	Player, Team	Pts./Avg.
1946–47	Joe Fulks, Philadelphia	1,389
1947–48	Max Zaslofsky, Chicago	1,007
1948–49	George Mikan, Minneapolis	1,698
1949–50	George Mikan, Minneapolis	1,865
1950–51	George Mikan, Minneapolis	1,932
1951–52	Paul Arizin, Philadelphia	1,674
1952–53	Neil Johnston, Philadelphia	1,564
1953–54	Neil Johnston, Philadelphia	1,759
1954–55	Neil Johnston, Philadelphia	1,631
1955–56	Bob Pettit, St. Louis	1,849
1956–57	Paul Arizin, Philadelphia	1,817
1957–58	George Yardley, Detroit	2,001
1958–59	Bob Pettit, St. Louis	2,105
1959–60	Wilt Chamberlain, Philadelphia	2,707

NBA Scoring Champions (continued)

Season	Player, Team	Pts./Avg.
1960–61	Wilt Chamberlain, Philadelphia	3,033
1961–62	Wilt Chamberlain, Philadelphia	4,029
1962–63	Wilt Chamberlain, San Francisco	3,586
1963–64	Wilt Chamberlain, San Francisco	2,948
1964–65	Wilt Chamberlain, S.F.–Phila.	2,534
1965–66	Wilt Chamberlain, Philadelphia	2,649
1966–67	Rick Barry, San Francisco	2,775
1967–68	Dave Bing, Detroit	2,142
1968–69	Elvin Hayes, San Diego	2,327
1969–70	Jerry West, Los Angeles	31.2
1970–71	Kareem Abdul–Jabbar, Milwaukee	31.7
1971–72	Kareem Abdul–Jabbar, Milwaukee	34.8
1972–73	Nate Archibald, Kansas City–Omaha	34.0
1973–74	Bob McAdoo, Buffalo	30.6
1974–75	Bob McAdoo, Buffalo	34.5
1975–76	Bob McAdoo, Buffalo	31.1
1976–77	Pete Maravich, New Orleans	31.1
1977–78	George Gervin, San Antonio	27.2
1978–79	George Gervin, San Antonio	29.6
1979–80	George Gervin, San Antonio	33.1
1980–81	Adrian Dantley, Utah	30.7
1981–82	George Gervin, San Antonio	32.3
1982–83	Alex English, Denver	28.4
1983–84	Adrian Dantley, Utah	30.6
1984–85	Bernard King, New York	32.9
1985–86	Dominique Wilkins, Atlanta	30.3
1986–87	Michael Jordan, Chicago	37.1
1987–88	Michael Jordan, Chicago	35.0
1988–89	Michael Jordan, Chicago	32.5
1989–90	Michael Jordan, Chicago	33.6
1990–91	Michael Jordan, Chicago	31.5
1991–92	Michael Jordan, Chicago	30.1
1992–93	Michael Jordan, Chicago	32.6
1993–94	David Robinson, San Antonio	29.8
1994–95	Shaquille O'Neal, Orlando	29.3
1995–96	Michael Jordan, Chicago	30.4
1996–97	Michael Jordan, Chicago	29.6

JOE FULKS: THE NBA'S FIRST SCORING CHAMPION

"Jumpin' Joe" Fulks, the NBA's first scoring champion, was one of the founding fathers of the exciting, freewheeling modern game of basketball. Using a one-handed jump shot that was revolutionary for his time, Fulks scored 1,389 points and averaged 23.2 points per game in 1946–47, the first season of the Basketball Association of America, the NBA's forerunner. No other player reached 1,000 points or averaged as many as 17 per game.

Fulks' acrobatic jumpers brought a new dimension to pro basketball and helped the NBA get off the ground. "He could shoot from anyplace," said longtime Celtics coach Red Auerbach. "We set up our defenses to revolve around him."

Joe Fulks became the NBA's first scoring champion. His trademark one-handed jumper devastated defenses.

On February 10, 1949, Fulks set an NBA record by scoring 63 points in a single game, about as much as entire teams produced in the era before the 24-second shot clock. His offensive skill drew comparisons to baseball's Babe Ruth, who early in his career often hit more home runs in a season than did entire baseball teams.

"Joe was one of the game's pioneers," said Eddie Gottlieb, who coached and later owned the Philadelphia Warriors, for whom Fulks played for eight seasons. "He had the greatest assortment of shots I've ever seen in basketball—then, now or who knows when."

Although he didn't invent the jump shot, Fulks was one of the first to use it successfully. Unlike today's shooters, who are taught to square up facing the basket before firing, Fulks would leave the ground and spin in either direction before launching his shot, sometimes switching the ball from one hand to another while in mid-air. He also excelled at firing turnaround jumpers and shooting with either hand while on the run.

But he did more than shoot, even though he was relatively slow-footed and not the best defender. "Everyone remembers him for his outstanding ability as a shooter," said teammate Paul Arizin, "but Joe could do other things. He was a tremendous defensive rebounder and a hard worker every second he was on the floor."

Did you know? Joe Fulks played in the first two NBA All-Star Games, in 1951 and 1952.

THE NBA'S CLOSEST SCORING RACE

George Gervin and David Thompson were two of the brightest stars in the American Basketball Association, the league that existed from 1967 to

A 73-point effort by **David Thompson** was not enough to win him the scoring title.

1976 and was best known for its red, white, and blue basketballs. Both players were just reaching the height of their skills when their teams entered the NBA, and in 1977–78 they competed in the closest NBA scoring race ever, a race that came down to the final day of the season.

Going into each team's final game, the 6' 7" Gervin led the 6' 4" Thompson by only hundredths of a point per game. Thompson's Denver Nuggets were in Detroit for an afternoon game against the Pistons, while Gervin's San Antonio Spurs were in New Orleans to face the Jazz in a night game. That difference, giving Gervin last licks, would prove important. And since neither game meant anything in the playoff races, all eyes were focused on the individual scoring duel.

From the start of the Denver-Detroit game, it was clear the Nuggets would do everything they could to help Thompson. They constantly passed him the ball and urged him to shoot. They even passed up shots of their own to give Thompson more opportunities to score.

Thompson came through with an NBA-record 32 points in the first quarter alone. He had 53 at halftime, and despite cooling off in the second half finished with 73 for the game, won by Detroit 139-137. Thompson's 73 points were the third-highest scoring total in NBA history. "I pushed it out pretty far with seventy-three," said Thompson. "I didn't think he'd be able to catch me. I remember M. L. Carr saying, 'Well, D, I think you got it. There's no way Gervin could get that many points.'"

Oh, no?

When he stepped onto the court at the Louisiana Superdome that night, Gervin knew exactly what he had to. If he scored 58 points or more, the scoring crown was his; anything less and he would finish second.

Like the Denver players did for Thompson, the Spurs kept feeding Gervin the ball and telling him to shoot. Gervin scored 20 points in the first quarter, then broke loose for 33 in the second period, erasing Thompson's single quarter scoring record after just seven hours and matching Thompson's 53 first-half points.

Two minutes into the third quarter, Gervin scored his 58th and 59th points to secure the scoring championship. He was removed from the game to a standing ovation. He played little after that and finished with 63 points in 33 minutes. The Spurs lost the game 153-132, but Gervin won the scoring title by averaging 27.22 points per game to 27.15 for Thompson.

"Me and my teammates had a great relationship and they pushed me over the top," said Gervin.

The 1977–78 scoring race served as a link between Gervin and Thompson throughout their careers. The link was strengthened in 1996, when the two stars were inducted together into the Basketball Hall of Fame.

The 10 Highest Scoring Games in NBA History

Wilt Chamberlain has recorded seven of the 10 highest-scoring games in NBA history, as the following list shows. Note that while his 100-point game was a home game for Philadelphia, it actually was played in Hershey, Pennsylvania, where the team played several games to try to attract additional fans.

10 Highest Scoring Games

Player, Team, and Opponent, Points, Date

Wilt Chamberlain, Philadelphia vs. New York, 100, 3/2/62
Wilt Chamberlain, Philadelphia vs. Los Angeles, 78, 12/8/61
Wilt Chamberlain, Philadelphia vs. Chicago, 73, 1/13/62
Wilt Chamberlain, San Francisco at New York, 73, 11/16/62
David Thompson, Denver at Detroit, 73, 4/9/78
Wilt Chamberlain, San Francisco at Los Angeles, 72, 11/3/62
Elgin Baylor, Los Angeles at New York, 71, 11/15/60
David Robinson, San Antonio at L.A. Clippers, 71, 4/24/94
Wilt Chamberlain, San Francisco at Syracuse, 70, 3/10/93
Michael Jordan, Chicago at Cleveland, 69, 3/28/90

Wilt Scores 100

It's the greatest scoring game in NBA history, a record that is not likely to be broken. On March 2, 1962, Wilt Chamberlain of the Philadelphia Warriors scored an even 100 points as the Warriors

Wilt Chamberlain
receives congratulations from teammates and fans after he scored his 100th point of the game.

defeated the New York Knicks 169-147 before 4,124 fans at the Hershey, Pennsylvania, Fairgrounds.

When the Philadelphia players were walking to the arena, they passed a shooting gallery in the Fairgrounds. Chamberlain picked up a rifle, took aim at the moving ducks, and didn't miss a single one. Right then and there, the Knicks should have known they were in for a long night.

New York was without its starting center, Phil Jordan, who did not play because of the flu. Backup center Darrall Imhoff and forward Cleveland Buckner were helpless in trying to stop the 7' 1", 275-pound Chamberlain from scoring.

Chamberlain had 23 points in the first quarter and 41 at halftime, then added 28 in the third quarter for a total of 69. Announcer Dave Zinkoff began calling out Chamberlain's point total every time he scored, and the fans responded with a steady chant of "Give It to Wilt, Give It to Wilt!"

With five minutes left, Chamberlain was up to 89 points. The Knicks tried to stop the barrage by fouling other Philadelphia players as soon as they touched the ball, keeping it out of Chamberlain's hands. The Warriors countered by quickly fouling the Knicks to regain possession of the ball, so they could feed it to Chamberlain again.

Finally, with 46 seconds left, Chamberlain took a pass from Joe Ruklick and hit a short shot, and there it was—100 points. Fans raced onto the court and the game was stopped. Chamberlain went to the locker room, where Warriors PR man Harvey Pollack wrote the number 100 on a piece of paper and gave it to Chamberlain to hold up for photographers. Chamberlain finished his remarkable night shooting 36-for-63 from the field and, despite being a notoriously bad foul shooter, a record 28-for-32 from the line.

"As time goes by, I feel more and more a part of that hundred-point game," Chamberlain reflected more than three decades later. "It has become my handle, and I've come to realize just what I did. People will say to a little kid, 'See that guy right there? He scored one hundred points in a game.' I'm definitely proud of it."

Did you know? Wilt Chamberlain played 1,045 games during his NBA career and did not foul out of a single one.

Career Scoring Average Leaders

Player	G	FGM	FTM	Pts.	Avg.
Michael Jordan	848	10,081	6,233	26,920	31.7
Wilt Chamberlain	1,045	12,681	6,057	31,419	30.1
Elgin Baylor	846	8,693	5,763	23,149	27.4
Jerry West	932	9,016	7,160	25,192	27.0
Bob Pettit	792	7,349	6,182	20,880	26.4
George Gervin	791	8,045	4,541	20,708	26.2
Karl Malone	980	9,510	6,505	25,592	26.1
Oscar Robertson	1,040	9,508	7,694	26,710	25.7
David Robinson	563	5,087	4,168	14,366	25.5
Dominique Wilkins	1,047	9,913	6,002	26,534	25.3

Career Leaders

FIELD GOALS MADE

Player	FGM
Kareem Abdul-Jabbar	15,837
Wilt Chamberlain	12,681
Elvin Hayes	10,976
Alex English	10,659
John Havlicek	10,513
Michael Jordan	10,081
Dominique Wilkins	9,913
Robert Parish	9,614
Karl Malone	9,510
Oscar Robertson	9,508

FIELD GOALS ATTEMPTED

Player	FGA
Kareem Abdul-Jabbar	28,307
Elvin Hayes	24,272
John Havlicek	23,930
Wilt Chamberlain	23,497
Dominique Wilkins	21,457
Alex English	21,036
Elgin Baylor	20,171
Michael Jordan	19,793
Oscar Robertson	19,620
Moses Malone	19,225

FIELD GOAL PERCENTAGE (MINIMUM 2,000 MADE)

Player	FGM	FGA	Pct.
Artis Gilmore	5,732	9,570	.599
Mark West	2,491	4,264	.584
Shaquille O'Neal	3,760	6,513	.577
Steve Johnson	2,841	4,965	.572
Darryl Dawkins	3,477	6,079	.572
James Donaldson	3,105	5,442	.571
Jeff Ruland	2,105	3,734	.564
Kareem Abdul-Jabbar	15,837	28,307	.559
Kevin McHale	6,830	12,334	.554
Otis Thorpe	6,154	11,155	.552

FREE THROW SHOOTING

A player stands by himself, 15 feet from the basket, the ball in his hands. Everyone else is standing still, waiting. All eyes are on the player at the free throw line—will he make it or will he miss?

Shooting a foul shot may seem simple. There are no defenders guarding you, you can take your time and you can shoot the ball any way you like. You don't have to spin or jump to get your shot away; you can just stand there and shoot. Yet some of the greatest players in basketball history have been terrible free throw shooters. Wilt Chamberlain could not make half his free throw attempts, finishing his career with a .465 accuracy mark. Chamberlain once missed 22 free throws in a single game! Among today's players, Shaquille O'Neal is an All-Star, but not from the foul line—after five NBA seasons, his free throw percentage is only .537.

Other players take pride in excelling from the foul line. Hall of Famer Rick Barry, who played professionally from 1965 to 1980, used an underhanded shooting style that was popular decades earlier and used it well enough to make nine out of ten tries from the line. Barry's .900 mark was the best in NBA history until Mark Price came along. Price, who played nine seasons with the Cleveland Cavaliers before moving on to Washington and Golden State, now ranks number one at .907. Here are the rest of the free throw records.

Shaq's Foul Line Fiascos

Shaquille O'Neal's career free-throw percentage (.537) is actually lower than his field goal percentage (.577). The foul line is not his favorite place.

Regular Season

Most Free Throws Made in a Game: 28 by Wilt Chamberlain, Philadelphia vs. New York at Hershey, Pennsylvania, March 2, 1962, and by Adrian Dantley, Utah vs. Houston at Las Vegas, Nevada, January 4, 1984.

Most Free Throws Made in a Season: 840 by Jerry West, Los Angeles, 1965–66.

Most Free Throws Made in a Career: 8,531 by Moses Malone, 1976–95.

Most Consecutive Free Throws Made: 97 by Michael Williams, Minnesota, March 9 to November 9, 1993.

Most Free Throws Made, None Missed, in a Game: 23 by Dominique Wilkins, Atlanta vs. Chicago, December 8, 1992.

Playoffs

Most Free Throws Made in a Game: 30 by Bob Cousy, Boston vs. Syracuse, March 21, 1953.

Most Free Throws Made, None Missed, in a Game: 17 by Gail Goodrich, Los Angeles at Chicago, March 28, 1971, by Bob Love, Chicago at Golden State, April 27, 1975, and by Reggie Miller, Indiana at New York, April 30, 1993.

Career Free Throw Shooting

Player	FTM	FTA	Pct.
Mark Price	1,893	2,088	.907
Rick Barry	3,818	4,243	.900
Calvin Murphy	3,445	3,864	.892
Scott Skiles	1,548	1,741	.889
Larry Bird	3,960	4,471	.886
Bill Sharman	3,143	3,559	.883
Reggie Miller	4,034	4,597	.878
Ricky Pierce	3,346	3,819	.876
Kiki Vandeweghe	3,484	3,997	.872
Jeff Malone	2,947	3,383	.871

This Price Is Right

It's no surprise that Mark Price is skilled at a basketball fundamental like free throw shooting. His father coached the sport at Sam Houston State and Oklahoma and was an assistant coach with the Phoenix Suns.

Price always has been able to shoot, but despite a fine career at Georgia Tech, pro scouts questioned whether he was quick enough for the NBA and whether, at 6' 0" and 180 pounds, he was strong enough to survive. Price did more than survive—he thrived.

Drafted by the Dallas Mavericks in the second round in 1986, Price immediately was traded to the Cleveland Cavaliers, where he began his career behind John Bagley but soon became the team's starter. Although the Cavs drafted Kevin Johnson, another point guard, in 1987, Price remained the starter and Johnson was traded to Phoenix.

Price played nine seasons with the Cavaliers, and they qualified for the playoffs in seven of them. Cleveland won a franchise-record 57 games in 1988–89, when Price averaged 18.9 points and 8.4 assists per game and shot .901 from the free throw line, the first of seven years in which he would hit more than 90 percent.

Mark Price sinks his free throws more than nine out of every ten attempts. He rarely misses two in a row.

Price missed all but 16 games of the 1990–91 season due to a torn knee ligament, but he bounced back to lead Cleveland to another 57-win season the following year, averaging 17.3 points and 7.4 assists per game and leading the league by shooting .947 from the foul line. Price led the league again the following season with a .948 mark.

Traded to Washington in 1995, Price missed all but seven games due to an injured left foot. But in 1996–97, after signing with the Golden State Warriors, Price made his second successful NBA comeback, starting at point guard and leading the NBA in free throw shooting for the third time in his career, this time with a .906 mark.

Price's career free throw percentage of .907 is the best in NBA history, and he is the only player to make more than nine out of ten attempts for his career. He's also good at three-point shooting, with a career percentage of .407. Price won the Long Distance Shootout at All-Star Saturday in 1993 and again in 1994.

Did you know? Mark Price sang with a Contemporary Christian group called Mark Price and Lifeline.

Rick Barry's Underhand Style: It Looked Strange, but It Worked

Rick Barry always did things his own way—including free throw shooting. At a time when just about every player in the league shot overhanded and with one hand, Barry used the two-handed, underhand style of shooting that had been popular in earlier years.

A scoring machine who could drive to the hoop or stick a jumper from 25 feet, Barry was the only man ever to lead the NCAA, NBA, and ABA in scoring, tallying over 25,000 points in a pro career that included a dozen All-Star appearances. He helped keep the ABA in business in its early years and later carried a rather ordinary Golden State Warriors team to the NBA championship in 1975.

His pursuit of perfection helped make Barry the outstanding player he was. If there is one phase of the game in which practice can indeed make perfect it is foul shooting, and Barry was one of the all-time greats. When he retired in 1980, his .900 career free throw percentage was the best in NBA history.

But why did he choose to shoot the ball underhanded? "Because it works," Barry explained. "Using both hands gives you better control of the ball, and shooting it underhanded lets you get off a softer shot, which gives you more room for error. If your shot hits the rim, it has a better chance to go in if you put it up softly."

Being able to make nine out of ten from the line should be

enough to convince anyone, yet few NBA players chose to copy Barry's style of shooting and none use it today. "I know it looks funny," he said, "but it works. I've discussed it with other players, and it amazes me that they won't try it just because of the way it looks."

Did you know? Rick Barry was the Most Valuable Player of the 1975 NBA Finals, when the Golden State Warriors swept the Washington Bullets for the title.

FREE THROWS MADE

Player	FTM
Moses Malone	8,531
Oscar Robertson	7,694
Jerry West	7,160
Dolph Schayes	6,979
Adrian Dantley	6,832
Kareem Abdul-Jabbar	6,712
Karl Malone	6,505
Michael Jordan	6,233
Bob Pettit	6,182
Wilt Chamberlain	6,057

FREE THROWS ATTEMPTED

Player	FTA
Wilt Chamberlain	11,862
Moses Malone	11,090
Kareem Abdul-Jabbar	9,304
Oscar Robertson	9,185
Karl Malone	8,983
Jerry West	8,801
Adrian Dantley	8,351
Dolph Schayes	8,273
Bob Pettit	8,119
Walt Bellamy	8,088

THREE-POINT SHOOTING

How many points is a basket worth? James Naismith never thought about the question when he invented basketball in 1891, figuring that every time a ball went into the basket, one point would be awarded. It wasn't something to be concerned about, either, since it only happened once in his initial game.

But the sport's rapid growth led to the decision, in 1893, to award three points for a successful field goal attempt. Four years later, field goals were reduced to two points, and that's pretty much the way things stood for most of a century.

In 1961, the newly formed American Basketball League, looking to attract attention, awarded three points for any shot made from beyond an arc that was 25 feet from the basket. That league folded after a little more than one year, but the idea of a three-point field goal was revived in 1967 when the American Basketball Association (ABA) was formed. The ABA set its three-point distance at 22 feet from the basket in the corners and 23 feet, 9 inches at the top of the key.

The ABA referred to three-pointers as "home run shots," and they became almost as popular as the league's red,

Dale Ellis has canned more three-point shots (1,461) than any other player in NBA history.

white, and blue basketball. Louie Dampier of the Kentucky Colonels made the most threes in the ABA's nine-year existence, but nobody would match the day an obscure player named Les Selvage had for the Anaheim Amigos. On February 15, 1968, he attempted 26 three-pointers and connected on 10 of them.

The three-point shot died with the ABA in 1976, but it was reborn three years later when the NBA decided to try it out for a year, using the same distances the ABA had used. Chris Ford of the Boston Celtics hit the first three-pointer in NBA history late during the first quarter of the team's season opener, and Larry Bird of the Celtics hit one in overtime that was vital to the East winning the All-Star Game that year. The shot was popular with fans and players alike and was made permanent when the Rules and Competition Committee met the following year. It has been used with increasing frequency and effectiveness ever since.

The NCAA followed the NBA's lead and adopted the three-point rule for the 1986–87 season, although in both the pros and colleges the distances have varied over the years. The NBA experimented with a 22-foot arc before going back to its original distances, while the college line is 19 feet 9 inches away. The three-pointer is also used in international play, where the line is 20 feet, 6 inches from the basket.

Recognizing the popularity of the three-point shot, the NBA developed a long distance shooting contest that has been a popular feature of All-Star Saturday since its introduction in 1986. Bird won the first three events, while Craig Hodges also won three in a row and Mark Price won twice. Similar shootouts are held at other major basketball events at both the collegiate and professional levels. Following are various NBA three-point shooting records.

Regular Season

Most Three-Point Field Goals Made in a Game: 11 by Dennis Scott, Orlando vs. Atlanta, April 18, 1996.

Most Three-Point Field Goals Made in a Season: 267 by Dennis Scott, Orlando, 1995–96.

Most Three-Point Field Goals Made in a Career: 1,461 by Dale Ellis, 1983–97.

Steve Kerr is shown competing in the 1997 NBA 3-point shootout. Kerr won the event.

Most Three-Point Field Goals Made, None Missed, in a Game: 8 by Jeff Hornacek, Utah vs. Seattle, November 23, 1994, and by Sam Perkins, Seattle vs. Toronto, January 15, 1997.

Most Consecutive Three-Point Field Goals Made in a Season: 13 by Brent Price, Washington, January 15–19, 1996, and by Terry Mills, Detroit, December 4–6, 1996.

Most Consecutive Games with at Least One Three-Point Field Goal Made: 89 by Dana Barros, Philadelphia and Boston, December 23, 1994, through January 10, 1996.

Highest Three-Point Field Goal Percentage in a Season: .524 by Steve Kerr, Chicago, 1994–95.

Highest Three-Point Field Goal Percentage, Career: .477 by Steve Kerr, 1988–97.

Kerr Finds His Niche

Find a need and fill it. It's the formula for success in business, and it works in sports, too.

The Chicago Bulls were the best team in the NBA in the summer of 1993, coming off three consecutive championships. But they needed a shooter to replace John Paxson, who was retiring. They needed someone who could spot up behind the three-point line and hit the open jumper.

Steve Kerr, who had played for three teams in five quiet NBA seasons but had become a free agent, recognized that need and decided he was the man to fill it. "I knew John Paxson was thinking of retiring," he explained, "and that my game was similar to his. We're both good outside shooters with three-point range who are most effective when we can spot up, catch and shoot. I figured I could fill that role, so Chicago was the team I wanted."

Kerr signed with the Bulls on September 29, 1993. One week later, Michael Jordan complicated Kerr's master plan by announcing his retirement. Kerr was called on to play more than he expected—a career-high 2,036 minutes in 1993-94, after playing just 481 minutes the previous season. But he averaged a career-high 8.6 points per game, the first of four consecutive years in which the 6' 3" guard has scored at least eight points per game for the Bulls.

With Jordan's return in 1995, Kerr settled into his expected role as the Bulls' designated shooter. He's the man coach Phil Jackson turns to when he needs an extra shooter on the court, somebody who can provide an outside threat and take advantage when opponents double-team Jordan or Pippen. He played an important role as a key reserve on Chicago's record-setting 1995-96 team that went 72-10 en route to the championship.

Kerr, who shoots about one-third of his shots from behind the three-point arc, has twice led the league in three-point field goal percentage and at .477 is the NBA career leader in that category. His .524 mark in 1994-95 is the best single-season percentage in league history.

Did you know? Steve Kerr was born in Beirut, Lebanon, and his father, the head of the American University in Beirut, was killed by terrorists.

Three-Point Field Goal Percentage Leaders, Year by Year

The three-point field goal was adopted by the NBA for the 1979-80 season. Craig Hodges and Steve Kerr, both of whom have led the league twice, are the only players to have led the league more than once.

Three-Point Field Goal Leaders

Year	Player, Team	Pct.
1979–80	Fred Brown, Seattle	.443
1980–81	Brian Taylor, San Diego	.383
1981–82	Campy Russell, New York	.439
1982–83	Mike Dunleavy, San Antonio	.345
1983–84	Darrell Griffith, Utah	.361
1984–85	Byron Scott, L.A. Lakers	.433
1985–86	Craig Hodges, Milwaukee	.451
1986–87	Kiki Vandeweghe, Portland	.481
1987–88	Craig Hodges, Milwaukee-Phoenix	.491
1988–89	Jon Sundvold, Miami	.522
1989–90	Steve Kerr, Cleveland	.507
1990–91	Jim Les, Sacramento	.461
1991–92	Dana Barros, Seattle	.446
1992–93	B. J. Armstrong, Chicago	.453
1993–94	Tracy Murray, Portland	.459
1994–95	Steve Kerr, Chicago	.524
1995–96	Tim Legler, Washington	.522
1996–97	Glen Rice, Charlotte	.470

REBOUNDING

You can't score if you don't have the ball. Rebounding, or getting possession of the ball after missed shots, is one of the keys to success in basketball. Far more often than not, the team that wins the battle of the boards wins the game as well. Some great scorers are outstanding rebounders as well. Kareem Abdul-Jabbar is the NBA's all-time leading scorer and third-leading rebounder. Wilt Chamberlain is the leading rebounder in NBA history and ranks second in scoring. Elvin Hayes and Moses Malone also rank in the top five in both categories.

Other players specialize in rebounding—none more so than Dennis Rodman, the NBA's leading rebounder in each of the past six seasons. It's not unusual for Rodman to score 4 or 6 points in a game, while grabbing 15 or 20 rebounds. For his career, he's scored 6,225 points and hauled down 10,324 rebounds. Following are various NBA rebounding records.

Regular Season

Most Rebounds in a Game: 55 by Wilt Chamberlain, Philadelphia vs. Boston, November 24, 1960.

Most Rebounds in a Half: 32 by Bill Russell, Boston vs. Philadelphia, November 16, 1957.

Most Rebounds in a Quarter: 18 by Nate Thurmond, San Francisco at Baltimore, February 28, 1965.

Most Rebounds in a Season: 2,149 by Wilt Chamberlain, Philadelphia, 1960–61.

Most Rebounds Per Game in a Season: 27.2 by Wilt Chamberlain, Philadelphia, 1960–61.

Most Rebounds in a Career: 23,924 by Wilt Chamberlain, Philadelphia, 1959–73.

Most Rebounds Per Game in a Career: 22.9 by Wilt Chamberlain, Philadelphia, 1959–73.

Rodman Rebounds into the Spotlight

Dennis Rodman does two things better than anyone in the NBA: rebound and get attention for himself. Whether or not you like his distinctive personality, you must give Rodman credit for what he has accomplished. He was out of high school and working at odd jobs, including janitor in an airport, when he grabbed onto basketball as his ticket to a better life, even though he had never played high school basketball.

Dennis Rodman displays the form that has made him one of the NBA's greatest rebounders.

"I was only 5' 11" in high school," he said. "Right after that, for about three years I was working at odd jobs: a car dealership, at Southwestern Bell, even at the (Dallas–Fort Worth) airport as a janitor. " Having grown to 6' 8", Rodman enrolled in junior college, then transferred to Southeastern Oklahoma State, where in three years he averaged 25.7 points and twice led the National Association of Intercollegiate Athletics (NAIA) in rebounding.

From there it was on to the NBA, where he carved his niche as a defensive star and a tenacious rebounder. He has contributed to championship teams in Detroit and Chicago. He is a one-of-a-kind player who can change the course of a game without taking a single shot. "He never worried about his offense, but just every other little thing that got us wins," said his coach with the Detroit Pistons, Chuck Daly.

Rodman first led the NBA in rebounding in 1991–92, and he has topped the league for six consecutive years while playing for three teams—Detroit, San Antonio, and Chicago. Meanwhile, he has shown the same ingenuity, resourcefulness, and determination in creating a unique off-court personality for himself. A movie star, an author, and a true celebrity, Rodman might show up for a public appearance wearing anything from a tuxedo to a wedding gown. With Dennis Rodman, you never know what to expect off the court. But on the court, you can be sure of solid defense and strong rebounding.

Did you know? Dennis Rodman starred with Jean-Claude Van Damme in the 1997 action film *Double Team*.

Career Rebounding Leaders

Player	Rebounds
Wilt Chamberlain	23,924
Bill Russell	21,620
Kareem Abdul-Jabbar	17,440
Elvin Hayes	16,279
Moses Malone	16,212
Robert Parish	14,715
Nate Thurmond	14,464
Walt Bellamy	14,241
Wes Unseld	13,769
Jerry Lucas	12,942

Top Rebounding Games in NBA History

Wilt Chamberlain and Bill Russell, longtime rivals and two of the greatest centers in NBA history, monopolize the list of the 10 best single-game rebounding performances in NBA history. Chamberlain has six and Russell has four.

Top Rebounding Games

Player, Team, and Opponent, Rebounds, Date

Wilt Chamberlain, Philadelphia vs. Boston, 55, 11/24/60
Bill Russell, Boston vs. Syracuse, 51, 2/5/60
Bill Russell, Boston vs. Philadelphia, 49, 11/16/57
Bill Russell, Boston vs. Detroit at Providence, 49, 3/11/65
Wilt Chamberlain, Philadelphia vs. Syracuse, 45, 2/6/60
Wilt Chamberlain, Philadelphia vs. Los Angeles, 45, 1/21/61
Wilt Chamberlain, Philadelphia vs. New York, 43, 11/10/59
Wilt Chamberlain, Philadelphia vs. Los Angeles, 43, 12/8/61
Bill Russell, Boston vs. Los Angeles, 43, 1/20/63
Wilt Chamberlain, Philadelphia vs. Boston, 43, 3/6/65

Rebounding Leaders, Year by Year

Wilt Chamberlain won 11 rebounding titles, more than any other player, while Dennis Rodman and Moses Malone have won six apiece. Rebounding statistics were first kept in the 1950–51 season. Through 1968–69, the league rebounding champion was the player with the most total rebounds. Since then, it has been the player with the highest rebounds-per-game average.

Rebounding Leaders

Season	Player, Team	Rebs./Avg.
1950–51	Dolph Schayes, Syracuse	1,080
1951–52	Larry Foust, Fort Wayne, and Mel Hutchins, Milwaukee	880
1952–53	George Mikan, Minneapolis	1,007
1953–54	Harry Gallatin, New York	1,098
1954–55	Neil Johnston, Philadelphia	1,085
1955–56	Bob Pettit, St. Louis	1,164
1956–57	Maurice Stokes, Rochester	1,256
1957–58	Bill Russell, Boston	1,564
1958–59	Bill Russell, Boston	1,612
1959–60	Wilt Chamberlain, Philadelphia	1,941
1960–61	Wilt Chamberlain, Philadelphia	2,149
1961–62	Wilt Chamberlain, Philadelphia	2,052
1962–63	Wilt Chamberlain, San Francisco	1,946
1963–64	Bill Russell, Boston	1,930
1964–65	Bill Russell, Boston	1,878
1965–66	Wilt Chamberlain, Philadelphia	1,943
1966–67	Wilt Chamberlain, Philadelphia	1,957
1967–68	Wilt Chamberlain, Philadelphia	1,952
1968–69	Wilt Chamberlain, Los Angeles	1,712
1969–70	Elvin Hayes, San Diego	16.9
1970–71	Wilt Chamberlain, Los Angeles	18.2
1971–72	Wilt Chamberlain, Los Angeles	19.2
1972–73	Wilt Chamberlain, Los Angeles	18.6
1973–74	Elvin Hayes, Capital	18.1
1974–75	Wes Unseld, Washington	14.8
1975–76	Kareem Abdul-Jabbar, Los Angeles	16.9
1976–77	Bill Walton, Portland	14.4
1977–78	Len Robinson, New Orleans	15.7
1978–79	Moses Malone, Houston	17.6
1979–80	Swen Nater, San Diego	15.0
1980–81	Moses Malone, Houston	14.8
1981–82	Moses Malone, Houston	14.7
1982–83	Moses Malone, Philadelphia	15.3
1983–84	Moses Malone, Philadelphia	13.4
1984–85	Moses Malone, Philadelphia	13.1
1985–86	Bill Laimbeer, Detroit	13.1

Rebounding Leaders (continued)

Season	Player, Team	Rebs./Avg.
1986–87	Charles Barkley, Philadelphia	14.6
1987–88	Michael Cage, L.A. Clippers	13.0
1988–89	Hakeem Olajuwon, Houston	13.5
1989–90	Hakeem Olajuwon, Houston	14.0
1990–91	David Robinson, San Antonio	13.0
1991–92	Dennis Rodman, Detroit	18.7
1992–93	Dennis Rodman, Detroit	18.3
1993–94	Dennis Rodman, San Antonio	17.3
1994–95	Dennis Rodman, San Antonio	16.8
1995–96	Dennis Rodman, Chicago	14.9
1996–97	Dennis Rodman, Chicago	16.1

MOSES MALONE: THE RELENTLESS REBOUNDER

One of the game's all-time great centers, Moses Malone was the first player of recent years to jump directly from high school to the pros, joining the ABA's Utah Stars in 1974. His pro career lasted 21 years, during which time he played for ten teams, two in the ABA and eight in the NBA. Despite not playing college ball, Malone had no trouble adjusting to the pro game; he was a force in the final two years of the ABA and then a dominant NBA player for a dozen seasons.

Even though at 6' 10", he was not as tall as the game's other legendary centers, Malone used his strength and quickness to become a relentless rebounder. He led the NBA in rebounding six times and in offensive rebounding eight times, and his 6,731 offensive rebounds are the most in NBA history. He also was a solid scorer, using post moves and put-backs to average over 20 points per game for his career.

Malone's best seasons came in the late 1970s and early 1980s with the Houston Rockets, and in the mid-1980s with the Philadelphia 76ers. He was the NBA's Most Valuable Player in 1978–79, when he averaged a career-high 17.6 rebounds per game and

Moses Malone was a true warrior underneath the basket on both ends of the floor.

led the league in rebounding for the first time. Two years later he led a mediocre Houston team to the NBA Finals, where they were beaten by the Boston Celtics in six games.

After another MVP season for the Rockets in 1981–82, Malone moved on to Philadelphia, where he took a team that had reached the NBA Finals three times in the last six years and turned it into a champion. Malone provided rebounding and inside scoring, the only ingredients they were missing. They already had the game's premier star in Julius Erving, a great playmaker in Maurice Cheeks, an outstanding shooter in Andrew Toney, and a fine defender and all-around player in Bobby Jones.

With Malone averaging 24.5 points-per-game and a league-leading 15.3 rebounds per game, the 1982–83 Sixers compiled a 67-15 record, then went 12-1 in the playoffs, the best postseason record ever. They swept the Los Angeles Lakers in the NBA Finals, and Malone was the NBA Finals MVP as well as the regular season MVP.

After leaving Philadelphia in 1986, Malone played nine more seasons for five teams—Washington, Atlanta, Milwaukee, Philadelphia again, and San Antonio. He ranks in the NBA's all-time top 10 in games, minutes, points, rebounds, offensive rebounds, defensive rebounds, field goals made, field goals attempted, free throws made, and free throws attempted.

Did you know? Moses Malone holds the NBA career record for most consecutive games without fouling out—1,212, from January 7, 1978 until the end of his career in 1995.

ASSISTS

An assist is a pass that leads directly to a basket. It sounds simple, but few players excel at this phase of the game. It takes a special kind of player to have the ball in his hands and not look for his own shot but instead focus on getting the ball to his teammates. And a good assist man not only gets his teammates the ball but gets it to them when and where they can get off the kinds of shots they like.

This pass-first, shoot-second mentality is something scouts look for in evaluating college players as prospective NBA point guards. It is expected that players coming into the NBA will be able to shoot the ball, but finding players who are willing to pass the ball and actually enjoy passing the ball is something else.

An assist can come on a set play or a fast break. It can set up a slam dunk or a three-pointer. It can be a short interior pass in the lane that travels no more than a foot or two, or it can be a 90-foot heave from one end of the court to the other.

Often a team's best assist man is its point guard or primary ballhandler, but not always. When a team has a frontcourt player who has unusual court vision and passing ability, such as Larry Bird of the Boston Celtics during the 1980s, it adjusts its offense to take advantage of his skills and runs its offense through him.

Great assist men come in all sizes. The top two in NBA history, John Stockton and Magic Johnson, are striking examples— Stockton is 6' 1" and 175 pounds, while Johnson stood a full 6' 9" and played most of his career at 220 pounds. Here are the various NBA assists records.

Regular Season

Most Assists in a Game: 30 by Scott Skiles, Orlando vs. Denver, December 30, 1990.

Most Assists in a Half: 19 by Bob Cousy, Boston vs. Minneapolis, February 27, 1959.

Most Assists in a Quarter: 14 by John Lucas, San Antonio vs. Denver, April 15, 1984.

Most Assists in a Season: 1,164 by John Stockton, Utah, 1990–91.

Most Assists Per Game, Season: 14.5 by John Stockton, Utah, 1989–90.

Most Assists in a Career: 12,170 by John Stockton, 1984–97.

Most Assists Per Game, Career: 11.5 by John Stockton, 1984–97.

Playoffs

Most Assists in a Game: 24 by Magic Johnson, Los Angeles vs. Phoenix, May 15, 1984, and by John Stockton, Utah at Los Angeles, May 17, 1988.

Most Assists Per Game in One Series: 17.0 by Magic Johnson, Los Angeles vs. Portland, 1985.

A Blue Chip Stock

John Stockton came to the NBA from little-known Gonzaga University in his hometown of Spokane, Washington. Though he had averaged 20.9 points and 7.2 assists per game as a senior, when he was drafted on the first round by the Utah Jazz the choice was met by a chorus of yawns punctuated by an occasional boo.

He broke in behind an All-Star point guard, Rickey Green, getting little playing time as a rookie. He then shared the position for two years before his breakthrough 1987–88 season, when he led the NBA in assists for the first time with 13.8 per game. It would prove to be the start of a remarkable string of nine consecutive years in which Stockton led the league in assists, with averages ranging from 11.2 to 14.5 assists per game. No other player has ever led the NBA in any category for that many years in a row.

Stockton will forever be paired with the player the Jazz drafted one year after he joined the team, forward Karl Malone. For 12 seasons now, "Stockton to Malone" has been a happy refrain for Utah fans as the team has become one of the most successful in the NBA, both on and off the court. Stockton and Malone shared MVP honors at the 1993 All-Star Game at Salt Lake City.

Stockton is a remarkably durable for a player of his size. He has played all 82 games in every season except 1989–90, when he appeared in 78 games—so he has missed just four games in 13 seasons, playing 1,062 of a possible 1,066 games.

Stockton holds most of the assists records in the book, including the career mark, which he took from Magic Johnson on February 1, 1995, and has since extended to 12,170 assists. He also holds the NBA record for most assists in a season (1,164), highest assists average for a season (14.5 assists per game), and highest assists average for a career (11.5 assists per game). And by leading the league in assists for the ninth time in 1995–96, he sur-passed the record held by Bob Cousy.

A member of the Dream Teams that won Olympic gold medals in Barcelona in 1992 and Atlanta in 1996, Stockton is also a steady outside shooter who has extended his jumper to three-point range and a crafty defen-sive player who is the NBA's all-time leader in steals.

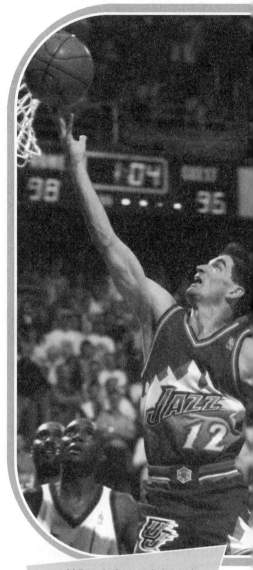

When he's not dishing the ball off to a teammate, **John Stockton** does the scoring himself.

Did you know? In 1988–89 and again in 1991–92, John Stockton led the NBA in steals as well as assists.

Career Assists Leaders

Player	Assists
John Stockton	12,170
Magic Johnson	10,141
Oscar Robertson	9,887
Isiah Thomas	9,061
Maurice Cheeks	7,392
Lenny Wilkens	7,211
Bob Cousy	6,955
Guy Rodgers	6,917
Mark Jackson	6,825
Nate Archibald	6,476

Simply Magic

Earvin "Magic" Johnson made millions of basketball fans world-wide by playing the game with skill and style and always keeping a smile on his face. "He had a passion, an incredible passion to play basketball," said Pat Riley, his longtime coach with the Lakers. "He wore this passion, this enthusiasm, on his sleeve. He let everyone know how happy he was to be playing this game."

At 6' 9", Johnson was a point guard in a power forward's body whose all-around excellence brought the term "triple-double" into the sport's language. No player Johnson's size had ever done the things he could do with a basketball. His height enabled him to see, pass, and shoot over defenders, while his quickness, agility, and skills baffled bigger opponents who tried to stop him.

"He defies the limits of traditional positions, because he can play any position," said Riley. And that's what he did as a rookie in Game 6 of the 1980 NBA Finals, when he moved from his usual guard spot to fill in for injured center Kareem Abdul-Jabbar and helped the Lakers beat Philadelphia 123-107 to wrap up the first of five titles they would win in the 1980s. Johnson's 42 points, 15 rebounds, and 7 assists ranks as one of the greatest playoff performances of all time.

For all his talent, Johnson also was a hard worker who made the most out of his skills. A weak shooter coming out of college, he made himself into one of the NBA's best. And he improved his ballhandling skills by countless hours of repetition while he was growing up. "I practiced all day," Johnson said. "I dribbled to the store with my right hand and back with my left. Then I slept with my basketball."

Johnson was an amazing passer and ranked as the NBA's career leader in assists until he was passed by John Stockton. Johnson dazzled fans and opponents with no-look passes, alley-oops, and spinning feeds, putting the spark in the Lakers' Showtime offense.

"The player I admired the most was Magic Johnson," said longtime foe Larry Bird of the Boston Celtics. "I've never seen anybody as good as him."

A three-time NBA Most Valuable Player, Johnson's rivalry with Bird won millions of new fans for the sport of basketball, and those fans were stunned in 1992 when Johnson announced he was retiring after having contracted the virus that causes AIDS. His subsequent work in promoting AIDS awareness and raising funds for research to fight the disease was widely praised. After brief comebacks as both a player and a coach, including playing in the 1992 All-Star Game and with the original Dream Team at the Barcelona Olympics, Johnson devoted his efforts to his business interests, which included opening entertainment centers in areas where they could serve largely African-American communities.

Did you know? Magic Johnson was named to the All-NBA First Team for nine consecutive seasons beginning in 1982–83.

Top Single-Game Assists Performances

Scott Skiles was the NBA's Most Improved Player for 1990–91, when he became the starting point guard for the Orlando Magic and increased his scoring from 7.7 to 17.2 points per game and his playmaking from 4.8 to 8.4 assists per game. Helping the latter was his 30-assist game against Denver on December 30, 1990, which broke the single-game NBA record of 29 established by Kevin Porter of New Jersey more than a decade earlier.

Assists Leaders

Year	Player, Team	Asst./Avg.
1946–47	Ernie Calverly, Providence	202
1947–48	Howie Dallmar, Philadelphia	120
1948–49	Bob Davies, Rochester	321
1949–50	Dick McGuire, New York	396
1950–51	Andy Phillip, Philadelphia	414
1951–52	Andy Phillip, Philadelphia	539
1952–53	Bob Cousy, Boston	547
1953–54	Bob Cousy, Boston	518
1954–55	Bob Cousy, Boston	557
1955–56	Bob Cousy, Boston	642
1956–57	Bob Cousy, Boston	478
1957–58	Bob Cousy, Boston	463
1958–59	Bob Cousy, Boston	557
1959–60	Bob Cousy, Boston	715
1960–61	Oscar Robertson, Cincinnati	690
1961–62	Oscar Robertson, Cincinnati	899
1962–63	Guy Rodgers, San Francisco	825
1963–64	Oscar Robertson, Cincinnati	868
1964–65	Oscar Robertson, Cincinnati	861
1965–66	Oscar Robertson, Cincinnati	847
1966–67	Guy Rodgers, Chicago	908
1967–68	Wilt Chamberlain, Philadelphia	702
1968–69	Oscar Robertson, Cincinnati	772
1969–70	Lenny Wilkens, Seattle	9.1
1970–71	Norm Van Lier, Cincinnati	10.1
1971–72	Jerry West, Los Angeles	9.7
1972–73	Nate Archibald, Kansas City, Omaha	11.4
1973–74	Ernie DiGregorio, Buffalo	8.2
1974–75	Kevin Porter, Washington	8.0
1975–76	Don Watts, Seattle	8.1
1976–77	Don Buse, Indiana	8.5
1977–78	Kevin Porter, Detroit, New Jersey	10.2
1978–79	Kevin Porter, Detroit	13.4
1979–80	Micheal Ray Richardson, New York	10.1
1980–81	Kevin Porter, Washington	9.1
1981–82	Johnny Moore, San Antonio	9.6
1982–83	Magic Johnson, Los Angeles	10.5

Assists Leaders (continued)

Year	Player, Team	Asst./Avg.
1983–84	Magic Johnson, Los Angeles	13.1
1984–85	Isiah Thomas, Detroit	13.9
1985–86	Magic Johnson, L.A. Lakers	12.6
1986–87	Magic Johnson, L.A. Lakers	12.2
1987–88	John Stockton, Utah	13.8
1988–89	John Stockton, Utah	13.6
1989–90	John Stockton, Utah	14.5
1990–91	John Stockton, Utah	14.2
1991–92	John Stockton, Utah	13.7
1992–93	John Stockton, Utah	12.0
1993–94	John Stockton, Utah	12.6
1994–95	John Stockton, Utah	12.3
1995–96	John Stockton, Utah	11.2
1996–97	Mark Jackson, Denver, Indiana	11.4

Top Single-Game Assists

Player, Team, and Opponent, Assists, Date

Scott Skiles, Orlando vs. Denver, 30, 12/30/90
Kevin Porter, New Jersey vs. Houston, 29, 2/24/78
Bob Cousy, Boston vs. Minneapolis, 28, 2/27/59
Guy Rodgers, San Francisco vs. St. Louis, 28, 3/14/63
John Stockton, Utah vs. San Antonio, 28, 1/15/81
Geoff Huston, Cleveland vs. Golden State, 27, 2/27/82
John Stockton, Utah at New York, 27, 12/19/89
John Stockton, Utah vs. Portland, 26, 4/14/88

Assists Leaders, Year by Year

John Stockton led the NBA in assists for nine consecutive seasons, one more than Bob Cousy. Oscar Robertson led the NBA in assists six times, though not consecutively. Through 1968–69, the NBA assists champion was the player with the most total assists. After that, it went to the player with the highest assists-per-game average.

Bob Cousy led the NBA in assists for eight straight seasons (1952–53 through 1959–60).

SEASONS, GAMES, AND MINUTES PLAYED

If there is one thing a coach likes, it's a player who comes to play every game. Coaches crave players they can rely on, players they can put out on the court and know they'll get 35 or 40 minutes of honest effort.

Today's NBA players average fewer minutes per game than their counterparts from the 1950s, 1960s, or 1970s. Coaches are more likely to rest even their best players for a few minutes in each half, preferring to use a fresh man off the bench rather than keep a tired starter on the court. Also, players are more likely to spend time on the bench with minor injuries because in the early years, players commonly played despite minor aches and pains, even though doing so may have risked making the injuries worse. That was just the way the game was played back then.

CAREER GAMES PLAYED LEADERS

Player	Games
Robert Parish	1,611
Kareem Abdul-Jabbar	1,560
Moses Malone	1,329
Elvin Hayes	1,303
John Havlicek	1,270
Buck Williams	1,266
Paul Silas	1,254
Alex English	1,193
James Edwards	1,168
Tree Rollins	1,156

CAREER MINUTES PLAYED LEADERS

Player	Minutes
Kareem Abdul-Jabbar	57,446
Elvin Hayes	50,000
Wilt Chamberlain	47,859
John Havlicek	46,471
Robert Parish	45,704
Moses Malone	45,071
Oscar Robertson	43,866
Buck Williams	41,726
Bill Russell	40,726
Hal Greer	39,788

The Chief Rules

Talent, conditioning, perseverance, and durability enabled Robert Parish to do something no other player in NBA history has been able to do—play 21 seasons. The first-round pick of the Golden State Warriors in 1976, Parish completed his 21st NBA campaign in 1996–97, helping the Chicago Bulls to a 69-13 record, the best in the league.

One of the most reliable scorers and rebounders in NBA history, the 7' 1" Parish played 14 seasons with the Boston Celtics, helping them to championships in 1981, 1984, and 1986. More than a decade later, he won another championship ring with the Bulls in 1997.

Parish was nicknamed "Chief" by Celtic teammate Cedric Maxwell after the Chief Bromden character in the film *One Flew Over the Cuckoo's Nest.* His chiseled features and stoic demeanor on the court set him apart from other players, but over the years he became a fan favorite in Boston where cries of "Chief! Chief!" were often heard rolling from the rafters at Boston Garden.

Did you know? Robert Parish appeared in nine All-Star Games, scoring 21 points in 1982 and grabbing 15 rebounds in 1984.

Robert Parish retired following the 1996–97 season. The star center played for 21 years in the NBA.

STEALS

As interest in pro basketball grew, so too did an appreciation for the defensive aspects of the game. Fans began to see what coaches have known all along— stopping a man from scoring is just as important as scoring yourself. Good defense may not get the headlines, but it wins games—in basketball as in any other sport.

In 1973–74, the NBA began keeping track of steals. Not surprisingly, most NBA records for steals are held by guards. However, the record for most steals in a single NBA game is held by a forward, and one who was known more for his scoring than his defense. On December 26, 1976, Larry Kenon, a lean, 6' 9" forward who played three seasons in the ABA and seven in the NBA, made 11 steals for the San Antonio Spurs against the Kansas City Kings. There have been 15 games in which a player got 10 steals, and all of them were by guards, but no one has beaten Kenon's 11. Following are various records for steals.

Regular Season

Most Steals in a Game: 11 by Larry Kenon, San Antonio at Kansas City, December 26, 1976.

Most Steals in a Half: 8 by eight players, most recently by Michael Jordan, Chicago at Boston, November 9, 1988.

Most Steals in a Quarter: 8 by Lafayette "Fat" Lever, Denver vs. Indiana, March 9, 1985.

Most Steals in a Season: 301 by Alvin Robertson, San Antonio, 1985–86.

Most Steals Per Game in a Season: 3.67 by Alvin Robertson, San Antonio, 1985–86.

Most Steals in a Career: 2,531 by John Stockton, Utah, 1984–97.

Most Steals Per Game in a Career: 2.71 by Alvin Robertson, 1984–96.

Playoffs

Most Steals in a Game: 8 by seven players, most recently by Mookie Blaylock, Atlanta vs. Indiana, April 29, 1996.

Most Steals in a Career: 358 by Magic Johnson, 1979–96.

Master Thief

Alvin Robertson was the NBA's most feared defensive player in the late 1980s and into the 1990s. First with San Antonio and later with Milwaukee, the 6' 4" Robertson used to drive opponents crazy with his lightning quick hands and feet, keeping them off balance and preventing them from running their offenses.

Robertson, who led the league in steals three times, could also hurt an opponent at the other end of the court. He scored over 17 points per game in four separate seasons, and in 1986 he did something that has only been done four times in NBA history. He recorded a quadruple double, reaching double figures in four statistical categories in the same game, getting 20 points, 10 assists, 11 rebounds, and 10 steals.

Alvin Robertson drives to the basket for the Toronto Raptors. Robertson was a tough player to contain with the ball, but he could be a menace even when he didn't have it.

Robertson, who had strength to complement his quickness, was a reserve guard with the San Antonio Spurs as a rookie in 1984–85. But the following season he started all 82 games and set NBA records with 301 steals and 3.67 steals per game and was voted the NBA's Defensive Player of the Year.

Robertson led the league twice more in assists during his career, which included five seasons in San Antonio, three with Milwaukee, one split between Milwaukee and Detroit, and after two years out of the game, a one-year comeback with Toronto. Beginning with 1985–86, he averaged 238 steals a year for seven years as one of the league's defensive standouts.

Robertson is one of only 13 players to get 10 or more steals in a single game, and the only one to do it more than once. He had 10 steals in a game four times during his career. He is one of only four men in NBA history to compile over 2,000 steals.

Did you know? Alvin Robertson was a teammate of Michael Jordan and Patrick Ewing on the U.S. Olympic team that won a gold medal in Los Angeles in 1984.

Steals Leaders, Year by Year

Steals have been kept as an official statistical category since the 1973–74 season. Michael Jordan, Alvin Robertson, and Micheal Ray Richardson each have led the league three times.

Career Steals Leaders

Player	Steals
John Stockton	2,531
Maurice Cheeks	2,310
Michael Jordan	2,165
Alvin Robertson	2,112
Clyde Drexler	2,081
Isiah Thomas	1,861
Derek Harper	1,841
Hakeem Olajuwon	1,811
Magic Johnson	1,724
Scottie Pippen	1,692

Steals Leaders

Year	Player, Team	Avg.
1973–74	Larry Steele, Portland	2.68
1974–75	Rick Barry, Golden State	2.85
1975–76	Don Watts, Seattle	3.18
1976–77	Don Buse, Indiana	3.47

Year	Player, Team	Avg.
1977–78	Ron Lee, Phoenix	2.74
1978–79	M. L. Carr, Detroit	2.46
1979–80	Micheal Ray Richardson, New York	3.23
1980–81	Magic Johnson, Los Angeles	3.43
1981–82	Magic Johnson, Los Angeles	2.67
1982–83	Micheal Ray Richardson, G.S.–N.J.	2.84
1983–84	Rickey Green, Utah	2.65
1984–85	Micheal Ray Richardson, New Jersey	2.96
1985–86	Alvin Robertson, San Antonio	3.67
1986–87	Alvin Robertson, San Antonio	3.21
1987–88	Michael Jordan, Chicago	3.16
1988–89	John Stockton, Utah	3.21
1989–90	Michael Jordan, Chicago	2.77
1990–91	Alvin Robertson, Milwaukee	3.04
1991–92	John Stockton, Utah	2.98
1992–93	Michael Jordan, Chicago	2.83
1993–94	Nate McMillan, Seattle	2.96
1994–95	Scottie Pippen, Chicago	2.94
1995–96	Gary Payton, Seattle	2.85
1996–97	Mookie Blaylock, Atlanta	2.72

BLOCKED SHOTS

Shotblocking has always been an important part of professional basketball. Bill Russell was the shotblocking center who anchored the NBA's greatest dynasty, the Boston Celtics teams that won 11 championships in 13 seasons from 1956–57 through 1968–69. Russell's effectiveness, along with that of other great centers like Wilt Chamberlain and Nate Thurmond, goes forever unmeasured, however, since the NBA did not start keeping track of blocked shots until the 1973–74 seasons. Since that time, great centers like Kareem Abdul-Jabbar, Hakeem Olajuwon, Patrick Ewing, David Robinson, and Dikembe Mutombo have been among the NBA's best shotblockers, along with defensive specialists like Manute Bol, Mark Eaton, and Elmore Smith.

Smith had the best shotblocking game in NBA annals in 1973, when he rejected 17 shots for the Los Angeles Lakers against the Portland Trail Blazers. Smith played eight seasons for four different teams during his NBA career, averaging double figures in both points and rebounds in each of his first five seasons.

Eaton, the 7' 4", 290-pounder who played 11 seasons for the Utah Jazz from 1982–93, had the best single season when it comes to blocking shots. In 1984–85, his third year in the league, he blocked 456 shots for an average of 5.56 per game, both NBA records. While centers like Russell and Olajuwon used their mobility and agility to block shots, Eaton relied on his size, getting position in the lane near his defensive basket and daring opposing players to try to drive at him. Here are all the shotblocking records.

Regular Season

Most Blocked Shots in a Game: 17 by Elmore Smith, Los Angeles vs. Portland, October 28, 1973.

Most Blocked Shots in a Half: 11 by Elmore Smith, Los Angeles vs. Portland, October 28, 1973, by George Johnson, San Antonio vs. Golden State, February 24, 1981, and by Manute Bol, Washington vs. Milwaukee, December 12, 1985.

Most Blocked Shots in a Quarter: 8 by Manute Bol, Washington vs. Milwaukee, December 12, 1985, and by Manute Bol, Washington vs. Indiana, February 26, 1987.

Most Blocked Shots in a Season: 456 by Mark Eaton, Utah, 1984–85.

Most Blocked Shots Per Game in a Season: 5.56 by Mark Eaton, Utah, 1984–85.

Most Blocked Shots in a Career: 3,363 by Hakeem Olajuwon, Houston, 1984–97.

Most Blocked Shots Per Game in a Career: 3.57 by David Robinson, San Antonio, 1989–97.

Olajuwon Makes Up for Lost Time

Hakeem Olajuwan poses a big problem for shooters when he's down in the paint. His quickness and jumping ability as a center enable him to swat away shots headed for the basket.

Hakeem Olajuwon grew up in Nigeria and played soccer and team handball as a boy. He didn't pick up a basketball until he was 15, but after he was spotted by a touring coach from the United States, he quickly took to the sport, absorbing it like a sponge. From the time he came to the United States to attend the University of Houston, he worked tirelessly to learn the subtleties of the game of basketball and develop the skills to become one of the greatest centers of all time.

"He just had a yearning to get better," said former NBA player and coach John Lucas, a teammate of Olajuwon's for three seasons with the Houston Rockets. "He practiced every day as if it was the last day. He brought a different intensity level to the game that only a few great players do."

Olajuwon, who stands closer to 6' 10" than his listed height of 7' 0", is a remarkably agile athlete who became an All-American by the age of 21 and the NBA's Most Valuable Player at 31. His youth training as a soccer goalie helped give him the footwork and agility to balance his size and strength, which enabled him to become one of the game's most complete big men. He has a tremendous assortment of spin moves around the basket, including an unstoppable baseline jumper, and he is comfortable taking jump shots from 18 feet out.

Defensively, Olajuwon uses his quickness and agility to great advantage, blocking shots of opposing centers and any player who tries to drive the lane against him. Besides averaging over 20 points and 10 rebounds per game for his career, Olajuwon has averaged about 260 blocks per season as well.

In college Olajuwon led the University of Houston to the CAA Final Four in each of his three varsity seasons as a member of the Cougars' "Phi Slamma Jamma" fraternity of dunk that also included Clyde Drexler and Larry Micheaux. In 1983–84 he averaged 16.8 points and led the NCAA in rebounding (13.5 rebounds per game), blocked shots (5.6 per game), and field goal percentage (.675), and was the top overall pick in the NBA Draft, going two slots ahead of Michael Jordan.

On the Houston Rockets, he joined 7' 4" Ralph Sampson in a Twin Towers alignment that carried the team to the NBA Finals in 1986. Olajuwon led the NBA in rebounding in 1988–89 and 1989–90 and in blocked shots in 1989–90 and 1992–93. But his biggest season was in 1993–94 when he led the Rockets to their first NBA championship and won Most Valuable Player, Defensive Player of the Year, and NBA Finals MVP honors. He was the NBA Finals MVP again in 1995 as the Rockets repeated as champions.

"It's an awesome experience just watching some of the things he can do on the court," said Rockets coach Rudy Tomjanovich. "He's a combination of quickness and finesse plus strength and power."

Did you know? Olajuwon's name translates into "always being on top."

Russell Made Defense Fashionable

Bill Russell changed the sport of professional basketball, proving that a player did not have to be a big scorer to dominate the game. Russell anchored basketball's most successful franchise, the Boston Celtics, leading them to 11 championships in his 13 years with the team and creating, from 1956–57 through 1968–69, the greatest dynasty in all of sports. His legacy was simple: Defense wins championships.

With Russell under the basket to cover up for any mistakes, the other Celtics players were free to guard their men more closely, to play the passing lanes and to gamble on making steals. The result was a tenacious team defense that was as responsible for Boston's success as any other factor, and the key to it all was Rus-

Bill Russell excelled at blocking shots. But even more impressive was his knack for rejecting a shot in the direction of a teammate so the Celtics would gain possession.

sell's shotblocking skills. "Nobody had ever blocked shots in the pros before Russell came along," said Red Auerbach, the longtime coach of the Celtics. "He upset everybody."

Russell was a winner at every level of the sport. In college, he teamed with K. C. Jones to lead the University of San Francisco to 55 straight wins and two NCAA titles. Then he led the United States to a gold medal in the 1956 Olympics in Melbourne. Auerbach traded to get Boston the rights to Russell, and although Russell missed the first third of his rookie season, he joined the Celtics in time to help them capture their first NBA title in 1956–57. The dynasty was off and running.

Russell never averaged as much as 20 points per game, but he averaged over 20 rebounds per game for 10 consecutive seasons. Unlike the big scorers, he did not need to have the ball in his hands to be effective. "There are two types of superstars," said Celtics teammate Don Nelson. "One makes himself look good at the expense of the other guys on the floor. But there's another type who makes the players around him look better than they are, and that's the type Russell was."

Russell's trademark was the blocked shot, and more often than not he would reject the opponent's attempt and direct the ball to a teammate so the Celtics would gain possession. Russell elevated the blocked shot into an art form and made it a psychological weapon, as he once explained: "A guy comes in and you block his shot, and you go down and get an easy layup. You might look at him and smile and say, 'Yes, we did that to you.' These things make statements."

At 6' 9" and 220 pounds, Russell was not an especially big center, but his quickness gave him an edge even against giants like 7' 1", 275-pound Wilt Chamberlain. Russell was an outstanding one-on-one defender, but he also used his agility and anticipation to switch off his man and block the shots of players driving the lane.

"He was the ultimate team player," said Boston guard Bob Cousy. "Without him there would have been no dynasty, no Celtics mystique."

Did you know? Bill Russell won the NBA Most Valuable Player award five times—and in three of those years he wasn't chosen to the All-NBA First Team. That's because the MVP was selected by the league's players in those days, while the All-NBA teams were picked by writers and broadcasters.

The NBA's Four Quadruple-Doubles

Only four players have been able to post quadruple-doubles—double figures in four of the five major statistical categories: points, rebounds, assists, steals, and blocked shots—in NBA history. They are:

Nate Thurmond, Chicago vs. Atlanta, Nov. 18, 1974: 22 points, 14 rebounds, 13 assists, 12 blocks

Alvin Robertson, San Antonio vs. Phoenix, Feb. 18, 1986: 20 points, 11 rebounds, 10 assists, 10 steals

Hakeem Olajuwon, Houston vs. Milwaukee, March 29, 1990: 18 points, 16 rebounds, 10 assists, 11 blocks

David Robinson, San Antonio vs. Detroit, Feb. 17, 1994: 34 points, 10 rebounds, 10 assists, 10 blocks

Mark Eaton led the NBA in blocked shots four out of five seasons from 1983 to 1988.

Blocked Shots Leaders, Year by Year

Kareem Abdul-Jabbar and Mark Eaton have led the league in blocked shots four times apiece, while George Johnson, Hakeem Olajuwon, and Dikembe Mutombo have each led the league three times. In fact, only 11 different players have led the league since blocked shots were first kept as an official statistical category in 1973–74.

Although Olajuwon has only led the league three times, he has blocked more shots than anyone in NBA history. Shawn Bradley, now with the Dallas Mavericks, led the blocks for the first time in 1997. At 7' 6", he may be the player to chase Olajuwon's record.

Career Blocked Shots Leaders

Player	Blocks
Hakeem Olajuwon	3,363
Kareem Abdul-Jabbar	3,189
Mark Eaton	3,064
Tree Rollins	2,542
Patrick Ewing	2,516
Robert Parish	2,361
Manute Bol	2,086
George T. Johnson	2,082
Larry Nance	2,027
David Robinson	2,012

Blocked Shots Leaders

Year	Player, Team	Avg.
1973–74	Elmore Smith, Los Angeles	4.85
1974–75	Kareem Abdul-Jabbar, Milwaukee	3.26
1975–76	Kareem Abdul-Jabbar, Los Angeles	4.12
1976–77	Bill Walton, Portland	3.25
1977–78	George Johnson, New Jersey	3.38
1978–79	Kareem Abdul-Jabbar, Los Angeles	3.95
1979–80	Kareem Abdul-Jabbar, Los Angeles	3.41
1980–81	George Johnson, San Antonio	3.39
1981–82	George Johnson, San Antonio	3.12
1982–83	Tree Rollins, Atlanta	4.29
1983–84	Mark Eaton, Utah	4.28
1984–85	Mark Eaton, Utah	5.56
1985–86	Manute Bol, Washington	4.96
1986–87	Mark Eaton, Utah	4.06
1987–88	Mark Eaton, Utah	3.71
1988–89	Manute Bol, Golden State	4.31
1989–90	Hakeem Olajuwon, Houston	4.59
1990–91	Hakeem Olajuwon, Houston	3.95
1991–92	David Robinson, San Antonio	4.49
1992–93	Hakeem Olajuwon, Houston	4.17
1993–94	Dikembe Mutombo, Denver	4.10
1994–95	Dikembe Mutombo, Denver	3.91
1995–96	Dikembe Mutombo, Denver	4.49
1996–97	Shawn Bradley, New Jersey–Dallas	3.40

COLLEGE RECORDS

College basketball is a passion shared by millions. It holds a unique place, combining the spirit and enthusiasm of high school basketball with a high skill level that approaches that of the pros.

In a sense, college basketball fans get the best of both worlds. And the excitement at a college game takes place off the court as well as on. Enthusiastic cheerleaders, blaring bands, students and alumni create a hoops hysteria unlike any other.

Each year, college basketball reaches a climax with March Madness, the NCAA Division I Basketball Championship that includes 64 of the top teams in the country. The tournament culminates in the NCAA Final Four, one of the hottest tickets in sports. Fans from the four schools good enough and fortunate enough to make it enjoy a three-day weekend of some of the most competitive and spirited basketball you'll ever want to see. Each year it's one of the highest rated sports events on television.

The college years are a special time for a basketball player, as for any young man or woman. They are a time of growing and maturing, a time for learning lessons in the classroom and on campus as well as on the court. They are a time when players come into their own and develop the skills and person-alities that will stay with them through their careers. It is at the college level that the best players really begin to test themselves, to face challenges and to make their mark in the sport they love.

The major governing body for college athletics is the NCAA, or National Collegiate Athletic Association. Colleges competing in basketball are grouped into divisions, so similarly sized schools may compete against each other for championships. The major schools, the basketball powers you see most often on TV, are in the NCAA's Division I. Since 1973–74, the NCAA has split smaller schools between Division II and Division III, the latter consisting of schools that do not award athletic scholarships. Small schools also may be members of the NAIA, or National Association of Intercollegiate Athletics, which has two divisions. Finally, junior colleges compete under the auspices of the National Junior College Athletic Association.

The tables of records in this chapter refer to those established by the major schools competing in the NCAA's Division I. Noteworthy records or achievements from other divisions are noted in text items or special charts. In the lists of championships, keep in mind that many schools have competed in different divisions of the NCAA and NAIA over the years. Also, note that women's college basketball is covered extensively in the chapter on women's basketball and thus not included here.

CHAMPIONSHIPS

NCAA Division I

The NCAA Division I men's basketball tournament has become one of the most popular and exciting sports events in the world, climaxing in the Final Four. UCLA has won the championship more often than any other school, capturing 11 titles— all but one of them from 1964 through 1975.

Since UCLA's dominance during the 1960s and 1970s, only five teams have claimed more than one NCAA championship. Indiana has won three titles ('76, '81, '87) and Kentucky ('78, '96), Louisville ('80, '86), North Carolina ('82, '93), and Duke ('91, '92) have all won two. Duke is the only school to win back-to-back titles since UCLA won seven straight from 1967 through 1973.

NCAA DIVISION I FINALS

Year	Championship Game, Final Four MVP
1939	Oregon 46, Ohio State 33, none selected
1940	Indiana 60, Kansas 42, Marv Huffman, Indiana
1941	Wisconsin 39, Washington State 34, John Kotz, Wisconsin
1942	Stanford 53, Dartmouth 38, Howard Dallmar, Stanford
1943	Wyoming 46, Georgetown 34, Ken Sailors, Wyoming
1944	Utah 42, Dartmouth 40 (OT), Arnie Ferrin, Utah
1945	Oklahoma State 49, NYU 45, Bob Kurland, Oklahoma State
1946	Oklahoma State 43, North Carolina 40, Bob Kurland, Oklahoma State
1947	Holy Cross 58, Oklahoma 47, George Kaftan, Holy Cross
1948	Kentucky 58, Baylor 42, Alex Groza, Kentucky
1949	Kentucky 46, Oklahoma State 36, Alex Groza, Kentucky
1950	CCNY 71, Bradley 68, Irwin Dambrot, CCNY
1951	Kentucky 68, Kansas State 58, none selected
1952	Kansas 80, St. John's 63, Clyde Lovellette, Kansas
1953	Indiana 69, Kansas 68, B. H. Horn, Kansas
1954	La Salle 92, Bradley 76, Tom Gola, La Salle
1955	San Francisco 77, La Salle 63, Bill Russell, San Francisco
1956	San Francisco 83, Iowa 71, Hal Lear, Temple
1957	North Carolina 54, Kansas 53 (3OT), Wilt Chamberlain, Kansas
1958	Kentucky 84, Seattle 72, Elgin Baylor, Seattle
1959	California 71, West Virginia 70, Jerry West, West Virginia
1960	Ohio State 75, California 55, Jerry Lucas, Ohio State
1961	Cincinnati 70, Ohio State 65 (OT), Jerry Lucas, Ohio State

NCAA Division I Finals (continued)

Year	Championship Game, Final Four MVP
1962	Cincinnati 71, Ohio State 59, Paul Hogue, Cincinnati
1963	Loyola (Ill.) 60, Cincinnati 58, Art Heyman, Duke
1964	UCLA 98, Duke 83, Walt Hazzard, UCLA
1965	UCLA 91, Michigan 80, Bill Bradley, Princeton
1966	UTEP 72, Kentucky 65, Jerry Chambers, Utah
1967	UCLA 79, Dayton 64, Lew Alcindor, UCLA (Kareem Abdul-Jabbar)
1968	UCLA 78, North Carolina 55, Lew Alcindor, UCLA (Kareem Abdul-Jabbar)
1969	UCLA 92, Purdue 72, Lew Alcindor, UCLA (Kareem Abdul-Jabbar)
1970	UCLA 80, Jacksonville 69, Sidney Wicks, UCLA
1971	UCLA 68, Villanova 62, Howard Porter, Villanova
1972	UCLA 81, Florida State 76, Bill Walton, UCLA
1973	UCLA 87, Memphis 66, Bill Walton, UCLA
1974	North Carolina State 76, Marquette 64, David Thompson, North Carolina State
1975	UCLA 92, Kentucky 85, Richard Washington, UCLA
1976	Indiana 86, Michigan 68, Kent Benson, Indiana
1977	Marquette 67, North Carolina 59, Butch Lee, Marquette
1978	Kentucky 94, Duke 88, Jack Givens, Kentucky
1979	Michigan State 75, Indiana State 64, Magic Johnson, Michigan State
1980	Louisville 59, UCLA 54, Darrell Griffith, Louisville
1981	Indiana 63, North Carolina 50, Isiah Thomas, Indiana
1982	North Carolina 63, Georgetown 62, James Worthy, North Carolina
1983	North Carolina State 54, Houston 52, Akeem Olajuwon, Houston (later, Hakeem Olajuwon)
1984	Georgetown 84, Houston 75, Patrick Ewing, Georgetown
1985	Villanova 66, Georgetown 64, Ed Pinckney, Villanova
1986	Louisville 72, Duke 69, Pervis Ellison, Louisville

Year	Championship Game, Final Four MVP
1987	Indiana 74, Syracuse 73, Keith Smart, Indiana
1988	Kansas 83, Oklahoma 79, Danny Manning, Kansas
1989	Michigan 80, Seton Hall 79 (OT), Glen Rice, Michigan
1990	UNLV 103, Duke 73, Anderson Hunt, UNLV
1991	Duke 72, Kansas 65, Christian Laettner, Duke
1992	Duke 71, Michigan 51, Bobby Hurley, Duke
1993	North Carolina 77, Michigan 71, Donald Williams, North Carolina
1994	Arkansas 76, Duke 72, Corliss Williamson, Arkansas
1995	UCLA 89, Arkansas 78, Ed O'Bannon, UCLA
1996	Kentucky 76, Syracuse 67, Tony Delk, Kentucky
1997	Arizona 84, Kentucky 79 (OT), Miles Simon, Arizona

NCAA Division I Tournament Records

Most Games Played in a Career: 23 by Christian Laettner, Duke, 1989-92.

Most Points in a Game: 61 by Austin Carr, Notre Dame vs. Ohio, 1970.

Most Points in a Series: 184 by Glen Rice, Michigan, 1989.

Most Points Per Game in a Series (minimum 3 games): 52.7 by Austin Carr, Notre Dame, 1970.

Most Points in a Career: 407 by Christian Laettner, Duke, 1989–92.

Most Points Per Game in a Career (minimum two years): 41.3 by Austin Carr, Notre Dame, 1969–71.

Most Three-Point Field Goals in a Game: 11 by Jeff Fryer, Loyola Marymount vs. Michigan, 1990.

University of Arizona's **Miles Simon** celebrates the Wildcats' 1997 NCAA championship game victory. Simon was named the MVP of the Final Four.

Most Three-Point Field Goals Without a Miss in a Game: 7 by Sam Cassell, Florida State vs. Tulane, 1993.

Most Three-Point Field Goals in a Series: 27 by Glen Rice, Michigan, 1989.

Most Three-Point Field Goals in a Career: 42 by Bobby Hurley, Duke, 1990–93.

Most Free Throws in a Game: 23 by Bob Carney, Bradley vs. Colorado, 1954.

Most Free Throws Without a Miss in a Game: 16 by Bill Bradley, Princeton vs. St. Joseph's, 1963, and by Fennis Dembo, Wyoming vs. UCLA, 1987.

Most Free Throws in a Career: 142 by Christian Laettner, Duke, 1989–92.

Highest Free Throw Percentage in a Career (minimum 30 free throws made): .957 by LaBradford Smith, Louisville, 1988–90.

Most Rebounds in a Game: 34 by Fred Cohen, Temple vs. Connecticut, 1956.

Most Rebounds in a Series: 97 by Elvin Hayes, Houston, 1968.

Most Rebounds in a Career: 222 by Elvin Hayes, Houston, 1966–68.

Most Rebounds Per Game
(minimum six games and two years): 19.7 by Johnny Green, Michigan State, 1957–59.

Most Assists in a Game: 18 by Mark Wade, UNLV vs. Indiana, 1987.

Most Assists in a Series: 61 by Mark Wade, UNLV, 1987.

Most Assists in a Career: 145 by Bobby Hurley, Duke, 1990–93.

Most Blocked Shots in a Game: 11 by Shaquille O'Neal, Louisiana State vs. Brigham Young, 1992.

Most Blocked Shots in a Career: 37 by Alonzo Mourning, Georgetown, 1989–92.

Most Steals in a Game: 8 by Darrell Hawkins, Arkansas vs. Holy Cross, 1993, and by Grant Hill, Duke vs. California, 1993.

Most Steals in a Series: 23 by Mookie Blaylock, Oklahoma, 1988.

Most Steals in a Career: 32 by Mookie Blaylock, Oklahoma, 1988–89, and by Christian Laettner, Duke, 1989–92.

Bill Bradley led the Princeton Tigers to the NCAA Tournament Final Four in 1965. Bradley was selected as the MVP of the tourney, even though Princeton did not participate in the championship game.

NIT

The National Invitation Tournament started one year before the NCAA tourney. It was created in 1938 by a group of New York sportswriters in an effort to crown a national champion, and it was staged at Madison Square Garden. It was such a success that the NCAA started its own tournament the following year, but the NIT was considered the more important event until the mid-1950s, when the NCAA began pressuring all conference champions to participate in its own tournament. The two tournaments competed for teams and popularity through the 1960s, but with the huge growth of the NCAA tournament since then, the NIT has dropped to secondary status, drawing teams which fail to receive NCAA bids.

NIT FINALS

Year	Championship Game, Tournament MVP
1938	Temple 60, Colorado 36, Don Shields, Temple
1939	Long Island U. 44, Loyola (Ill.) 32 , Bill Lloyd, St. John's
1940	Colorado 51, Duquesne 40, Bob Doll, Colorado
1941	Long Island U. 56, Ohio U. 52, Frank Baumholtz, Ohio
1942	West Virginia 47, Western Kentucky 45, Rudy Baric, West Virginia
1943	St. John's 48, Toledo 27, Harry Boykoff, St. John's
1944	St. John's 47, DePaul 39, Bill Kotsores, St. John's
1945	DePaul 71, Bowling Green 54, George Mikan, DePaul
1946	Kentucky 46, Rhode Island 45, Ernie Calverley, Rhode Island
1947	Utah 49, Kentucky 45, Vern Gardner, Utah
1948	St. Louis 65, NYU 52, Ed Macauley, St. Louis
1949	San Francisco 48, Loyola (Ill.) 47, Don Lofgan, San Francisco
1950	CCNY 69, Bradley 61, Ed Warner, CCNY
1951	Brigham Young 62, Dayton 43, Roland Minson, Brigham Young

Year	Championship Game, Tournament MVP
1952	La Salle 75, Dayton 64, Tom Gola & Norm Grekin, La Salle
1953	Seton Hall 58, St. John's 46, Walter Dukes, Seton Hall
1954	Holy Cross 71, Duquesne 62, Togo Palazzi, Holy Cross
1955	Duquesne 70, Dayton 58, Maurice Stokes, St. Francis (Pa.)
1956	Louisville 93, Dayton 80, Charlie Tyra, Louisville
1957	Bradley 84, Memphis 83, Win Wilfong, Memphis
1958	Xavier (Ohio) 78, Dayton 74 (OT), Hank Stein, Xavier
1959	St. John's 76, Bradley 71 (OT), Tony Jackson, St. John's
1960	Bradley 88, Providence 72, Lenny Wilkens, Providence
1961	Providence 62, St. Louis 59, Vin Ernst, Providence
1962	Dayton 73, St. John's 67, Bill Chmielewski, Dayton
1963	Providence 81, Canisius 66, Ray Flynn, Providence
1964	Bradley 86, New Mexico 54, Lavern Tart, Bradley
1965	St. John's 55, Villanova 51, Ken McIntyre, St. John's
1966	Brigham Young 97, NYU 84, Bill Melchionni, Villanova
1967	Southern Illinois 71, Marquette 56, Walt Frazier, Southern Illinois
1968	Dayton 61, Kansas 48, Don May, Dayton
1969	Temple 89, Boston College 76, Terry Driscoll, Boston College
1970	Marquette 65, St. John's 53, Dean Meminger, Marquette
1971	North Carolina 84, Georgia Tech 66 Bill Chamberlain, North Carolina
1972	Maryland 100, Niagara 69, Tom McMillen, Maryland
1973	Virginia Tech 92, Notre Dame 91 (OT), John Shumate, Notre Dame
1974	Purdue 97, Utah 81, Mike Sojourner, Utah

NIT Finals (continued)

Year	Championship Game, Tournament MVP
1975	Princeton 80, Providence 69, Ron Lee, Oregon
1976	Kentucky 71, UNC-Charlotte 67, Cedric Maxwell, UNC-Charlotte
1977	St. Bonaventure 94, Houston 91, Gary Sanders, St. Bonaventure
1978	Texas 101, North Carolina State 93, Jim Krivacs and Ron Baxter, Texas
1979	Indiana 53, Purdue 52, Butch Carter and Ray Tolbert, Indiana
1980	Virginia 58, Minnesota 55, Ralph Sampson, Virginia
1981	Tulsa 86, Syracuse 84 (OT), Greg Stewart, Tulsa
1982	Bradley 67, Purdue 58, Mitchell Anderson, Bradley
1983	Fresno State 69, DePaul 60, Ron Anderson, Fresno State
1984	Michigan 83, Notre Dame 63, Tim McCormick, Michigan
1985	UCLA 65, Indiana 62, Reggie Miller, UCLA
1986	Ohio State 73, Wyoming 63, Brad Sellers, Ohio State
1987	Southern Mississippi 84, La Salle 80, Randolph Keys, Southern Mississippi
1988	Connecticut 72, Ohio State 67, Phil Gamble, Connecticut
1989	St. John's 73, St. Louis 65, Jayson Williams, St. John's
1990	Vanderbilt 74, St. Louis 72, Scott Draud, Vanderbilt
1991	Stanford 78, Oklahoma 72, Adam Keefe, Stanford
1992	Virginia 81, Notre Dame 76, Bryant Stith, Virginia
1993	Minnesota 62, Georgetown 61, Voshon Lenard, Minnesota
1994	Villanova 80, Vanderbilt 73, Doremus Bennerman, Sienna
1995	Virginia Tech 65, Marquette 64 (OT), Shawn Smith, Virginia Tech
1996	Nebraska 60, St. Joseph's 56, Erick Strickland, Nebraska
1997	Michigan 82, Florida State 73, Robert Traylor, Michigan

Utah Loses NIT, Bounces Back to Win NCAA

In the 1940s, the NIT was the major event in college basketball, with the NCAA tournament second in importance. Neither tournament offered the schools much money in those days, but the NIT offered players a chance to visit New York, so teams with a choice often took the NIT over the NCAA. That's what the University of Utah did in 1944, choosing to compete in the NIT rather than the NCAA primarily because only two of its players had ever been to New York and the trip sounded appealing.

Utah promptly got beaten 46-38 by Kentucky in the first round of the NIT. Its players were all set to take the long train trip home when fate stepped in. The NCAA tournament had yet to begin, and Arkansas withdrew at the last minute after two of its players got hurt in a car accident. That left an opening in the field, and since Utah already was out of the NIT, the NCAA invited the Utes to be a last-minute replacement. Utah Coach Vadal Peterson put it to his players— would you rather stay in New York for a few days of sightseeing and then go home, or would you prefer to take a train to Kansas City for the NCAA Western bracket?

Reggie Miller dunks over J.R. Reid of North Carolina in a regular season game. Miller won the NIT Tournament MVP in 1985 when his UCLA Bruins defeated Indiana 65-62.

Bob Knight guided Indiana to a perfect season in 1976. Since then, no Division I team has finished a season undefeated.

"Let's go to Kansas City," said Utes star Arnie Ferrin. "Then we can return to New York (site of the NCAA championship game) and prove that our loss was a fluke."

So Utah became the first team to participate in both tournaments in the same season, and the Utes made the most of it. They beat Missouri and Iowa State to earn a trip back to New York, where they met Dartmouth in the title game. It was tight all the way, and though Utah led by four points going into the final minute, Dartmouth rallied to tie the score and send it into overtime. Four free throws by Ferrin in the extra period, giving him a game-high 22 points, helped the Utes to a 42-40 victory.

Utah had taken advantage of its second chance to win the NCAA title. And two nights later, in a charity game to benefit the Red Cross, it completed its comeback story by beating NIT champion St. John's 43-36.

After three weeks that hadbegun with a loss, Utah went home as champion after one of the greatest second-chance success stories in sports history.

UNBEATEN TEAMS

Twelve teams have enjoyed unbeaten seasons since 1937–38, the first year of national tournament competition.

Note: Both UCLA and North Carolina State went unbeaten in 1972–73 with UCLA winning the national championship. North Carolina State was on NCAA probation and thus ineligible to compete in the tournament.

Year	School	Record
1938–39	Long Island U.	23-0
1939–40	Seton Hall	19-0
1943–44	Army	15-0
1953–54	Kentucky	25-0
1955–56	San Francisco	29-0
1956–57	North Carolina	32-0
1963–64	UCLA	30-0
1966–67	UCLA	30-0
1971–72	UCLA	30-0
1972–73	North Carolina State	27-0
1972–73	UCLA	30-0
1975–76	Indiana	32-0

NCAA DIVISION II

Kentucky Wesleyan has won more Division II titles (six) than any other school in history, with Evansville next with five. Cal State-Bakersfield has won the title in three of the past five seasons.

Year	Champion
1956–57	Wheaton (Ill.)
1957–58	South Dakota
1958–59	Evansville
1959–60	Evansville
1960–61	Wittenberg
1961–62	Mt. St. Mary's (Md.)
1962–63	South Dakota State
1963–64	Evansville
1964–65	Evansville
1965–66	Kentucky Wesleyan
1966–67	Winston-Salem State
1967–68	Kentucky Wesleyan

Year	Champion (continued)
1968–69	Kentucky Wesleyan
1969–70	Philadelphia Textile
1970–71	Evansville
1971–72	Roanoke
1972–73	Kentucky Wesleyan
1973–74	Morgan State
1974–75	Old Dominion
1975–76	Puget Sound
1976–77	Tennessee–Chattanooga
1977–78	Cheyney State
1978–79	North Alabama
1979–80	Virginia Union
1980–81	Florida Southern
1981–82	District of Columbia
1982–83	Wright State (Ohio)
1983–84	Central Missouri State
1984–85	Jacksonville (Ala.) State
1985–86	Sacred Heart (Conn.)
1986–87	Kentucky Wesleyan
1987–88	Lowell (Mass.)
1988–89	North Carolina Central
1989–90	Kentucky Wesleyan
1990–91	North Alabama
1991–92	Virginia Union
1992–93	Cal State-Bakersfield
1993–94	Cal State-Bakersfield
1994–95	Southern Indiana
1995–96	Fort Hays State (Kan.)
1996–97	Cal State-Bakersfield

NCAA DIVISION III

North Park (Ill.) has won more NCAA Division III titles than any other school (five). They won three in a row from 1978–80, and claimed two more championships in 1985 and 1987.

Year	Champion
1974–75	Lemoyne–Owen (Tenn.)
1975–76	Scranton
1976–77	Wittenberg
1977–78	North Park (Ill.)
1978–79	North Park (Ill.)
1979–80	North Park (Ill.)
1980–81	Potsdam State (N.Y.)
1981–82	Wabash
1982–83	Scranton
1983–84	Wisconsin–Whitewater
1984–85	North Park (Ill.)
1985–86	Potsdam State (N.Y.)
1986–87	North Park (Ill.)
1987–88	Ohio Wesleyan
1988–89	Wisconsin–Whitewater
1989–90	Rochester (N.Y.)
1990–91	Wisconsin–Platteville
1991–92	Calvin (Mich.)
1992–93	Ohio Northern
1993–94	Lebanon Valley (Pa.)
1994–95	Wisconsin–Platteville
1995–96	Rowan (N.J.)
1996–97	Illinois Wesleyan

NAIA CHAMPIONS, DIVISION I

Oklahoma City has won four NAIA titles, all in the 1990s. Four teams have won three NAIA titles each: Grand Canyon, Hamline, Kentucky State, and Tennessee State.

Year	Champion
1936–37	Central Missouri State
1937–38	Central Missouri State
1938–39	Southwestern (Kan.)
1939–40	Tarkio
1940–41	San Diego State
1941–42	Hamline
1942–43	Southeast Missouri State
1943–44	no tournament due to World War II
1944–45	Loyola (La.)
1945–46	Southern Illinois
1946–47	Marshall
1947–48	Louisville
1948–49	Hamline
1949–50	Indiana State
1950–51	Hamline
1951–52	Southwest Missouri State
1952–53	Southwest Missouri State
1953–54	St. Benedict's (Kan.)
1954–55	East Texas State
1955–56	McNeese State
1956–57	Tennessee State
1957–58	Tennessee State
1958–59	Tennessee State
1959–60	Southwest Texas State
1960–61	Grambling State
1961–62	Prairie View A&M
1962–63	Texas–Pan American
1963–64	Rockhurst
1964–65	Central State (Ohio)
1965–66	Oklahoma Baptist
1966–67	St. Benedict's (Kan.)
1967–68	Central State (Ohio)
1968–69	Eastern New Mexico
1969–70	Kentucky State
1970–71	Kentucky State
1971–72	Kentucky State
1972–73	Guilford (N.C.)
1973–74	West Georgia
1974–75	Grand Canyon
1976–77	Texas Southern

Year	Champion (continued)
1975–76	Coppin State (Md.)
1979–80	Cameron (Okla.)
1980–81	Bethany Nazarene (Okla.)
1981–82	Spartanburg (S.C.)
1982–83	Charleston (S.C.)
1983–84	Fort Hays State (Kan.)
1984–85	Fort Hays State (Kan.)
1985–86	David Lipscomb (Kan.)
1986–87	Washburn (Kan.)
1987–88	Grand Canyon
1988–89	St. Mary's (Texas)
1989–90	Birmingham Southern
1990–91	Oklahoma City
1991–92	Oklahoma City
1992–93	Hawaii Pacific
1993–94	Oklahoma City
1994–95	Birmingham Southern
1995–96	Oklahoma City
1996–97	Life View (Ga.)

NAIA CHAMPIONS, DIVISION II

Since the NAIA Division II Championships began in 1991–92, no team located in the East or South has claimed a title.

Year	Champion
1991–92	Grace (Ind.)
1992–93	Willamette (Ore.)
1993–94	Eureka (Ill.)
1994–95	Bethel (Ind.)
1995–96	Albertson (Idaho)
1996–97	Siena Heights (Mich.)

INDIVIDUAL RECORDS

Scoring

Most Points in a Game: 100 by Frank Selvy, Furman vs. Newberry, February 13, 1954.

Most Points in a Game, vs. Division I Opponent: 72 by Kevin Bradshaw, U.S. International vs. Loyola Marymount, January 5, 1991.

Most Points in a Season: 1,381 by Pete Maravich, Louisiana State, 1969–70.

Highest Scoring Average in a Season: 44.5 points per game by Pete Maravich, Louisiana State, 1969–70.

Highest Scoring Average in a Career: 44.2 by Pete Maravich, Louisiana State, 1968–70.

Highest Field Goal Percentage in a Season: .746 by Steve Johnson, Oregon State, 1980–81.

Highest Field Goal Percentage in a Career: .685 by Steve Scheffler, Purdue, 1987–90.

Most Free Throws in a Game: 30 by Pete Maravich, Louisiana State vs. Oregon State, December 22, 1969.

Most Consecutive Free Throws Made: 64 by Joe Dykstra, Western Illinois, December 1, 1981, through January 4, 1982.

Most Free Throws in a Season: 355 by Frank Selvy, Furman, 1953–54.

Highest Free Throw Percentage in a Season: .959 by Craig Collins, Penn State, 1984–85.

Most Free Throws in a Career: 905 by Dickie Hemric, Wake Forest, 1952–55.

Highest Free Throw Percentage in a Career: .909 by Greg Starrick, Kentucky & Southern Illinois, 1969–72.

Most Three-Point Field Goals in a Game: 14 by Dave Jamerson, Ohio vs. Charleston, December 21, 1989, and by Askia Jones, Kansas State vs. Fresno State, March 24, 1994.

Most Consecutive Three-Point Field Goals: 15 by Todd Leslie, Northwestern, December 15–28, 1990.

Most Three-Point Field Goals in a Season: 158 by Darrin Fitzgerald, Butler, 1986–87.

Highest Three-Point Field Goal Percentage in a Season: .634 by Glenn Tropf, Holy Cross, 1987–88.

Most Three-Point Field Goals in a Career: 401 by Doug Day, Radford, 1990–93.

Most Consecutive Games with At Least One Three-Point Field Goal: 73 by Wally Lancaster, Virginia Tech, December 30, 1986, through March 4, 1989.

Highest Three-Point Field Goal Percentage in a Career: .497 by Tony Bennett, Wisconsin-Green Bay, 1989–92.

Pistol Pete: Flash and Fundamentals

He was known for his floppy socks and flamboyant style of play, but few were better schooled in the game of basketball than Pete Maravich. The son of a prominent coach, Maravich grew up with a basketball in his hands, dribbling it wherever he went. His father, Press Maravich, taught him correct fundamentals of the game at an early age, laying a solid foundation upon which Pete would build his flashy game. "My father was a strong believer in the basics," said Pete. "He wouldn't let me do anything fancy until I could do it right. All the moves you saw on the court were a result of many long hours of practice."

Maravich, who became known as "Pistol Pete" because of his shooting ability, starred at Louisiana State University, where his father was the head coach. Maravich led the nation in scoring in each of his three seasons of varsity ball (1968–70), joining the legendary Oscar Robertson (Cincinnati, 1958–60) as the only three-time NCAA Division I scoring champions.

Shot Out of a Pistol

After sitting out his freshman year, "Pistol" Pete Maravich led all Division I scorers for three straight seasons. A sharpshooter from the floor; Maravich still holds several college records.

A 6' 5" guard, Maravich was an outstanding shooter who could score from long range or by driving to the basket. He handled the ball as if it were tied to his hand with a string, dribbling between his legs and behind his back to get away from defenders and tossing no-look passes to open teammates when defenders double-teamed him. His flair for the game made him a fan favorite.

As a senior in 1970, Maravich rewrote the college basketball record book by scoring 1,381 points and averaging 44.5 points per game, both all-time records. In 10 games that season he scored 50 points or more, another NCAA record. And he did it before the NCAA had a three-point field goal rule.

Maravich went on to enjoy a solid NBA career, first with the Atlanta Hawks and later the New Orleans Jazz. He led the NBA in scoring in 1977 at 31.1 points-per-game and twice was voted to the All-NBA First Team. He completed his 10-year pro career in 1980 as a member of the Boston Celtics and retired with a career scoring average of 24.2 points-per-game.

Maravich died in 1988 at the age of 40 while playing the game he loved. He suffered a heart attack while playing a game of pickup basketball.

"Pete was ahead of his time, in so many ways," said Magic Johnson, a great guard who followed in Maravich's footsteps. "I look at videos of Pete and see him doing many of the things I did. He was a great player whose style made many fans for the game of basketball."

Maravich owns the top three single-season scoring averages in NCAA Division I history: 44.5 points per game as a senior, 44.2

points per game as a junior, and 43.8 points per game as a sophomore. And his record-setting career total of 3,667 points was accomplished in just three seasons, since freshmen were ineligible to compete on varsity teams when Maravich was in college. That means that Maravich scored more points in three seasons than any other player has been able to score in four.

Did You Know? Maravich scored 50 points or more 28 times during his college career, and 40 points or more 56 times.

NCAA Division I Top Games

Player, Team, and Opponent, Points, Date

Frank Selvy, Furman vs. Newberry, 100, 2/13/54
Paul Arizin, Villanova vs. Philadelphia, NAMC 85, 2/12/49
Freeman Williams, Portland State vs. Rocky Mountain, 81, 2/3/78
Bill Mlkvy, Temple vs. Wilkes, 73, 3/3/51
Kevin Bradshaw, U.S. International vs. Loyola Marymount, 72, 1/5/91
Freeman Williams, Portland State vs. Southern Oregon, 71, 2/9/77
Pete Maravich, Louisiana State vs. Alabama, 69, 2/7/70
Calvin Murphy, Niagara vs. Syracuse, 68, 12/7/68
Jay Handlan, Washington & Lee vs. Furman, 66, 2/17/51
Pete Maravich, Louisiana State vs. Tulane, 66, 2/10/69
Anthony Roberts, Oral Roberts vs. North Carolina A&T, 66, 2/19/77

Frank Selvy Scores 100

Only twice in history has a player scored as many as 100 points in a game between four-year colleges, and it happened just nine days apart. Barely more than a week after Bevo Francis scored 113 points for Rio Grande, Frank Selvy of Furman scored an even 100 on February 13, 1954.

The 6' 2" Selvy was a great jump shooter who, unlike Francis, played for a Division I school and would later have a solid pro career. When he left Furman he had scored 2,538 points in his career, at the time an NCAA record.

His 100-point game against Newberry came on Furman's home court, Textile Hall in Greenville, South Carolina. Selvy's mother had never seen her son play college ball, but she came to this game along with hundreds of fans from his hometown of Corbin, South Carolina. Selvy scored 24 points in the first quarter, and the man assigned to guard him, Bobby Bailey, fouled out after playing less than three minutes! Selvy added 13 points in the second quarter to set a school record of 37 points in one half. It was a record that would not last long.

Furman's **Frank Selvy** fights for a rebound during a 1954 game with LaSalle. Selvy remains the only player in NCAA Division I history to score 100 points in a game.

Selvy's coach, Lyles Alley, and his teammates decided to get him the ball every time they could in the second half. They urged him to shoot and passed up open shots of their own in order to give him more chances to score. Selvy responded by scoring 26 points in the third quarter, then getting 37 of his team's 40 points in the final period to finish with an even 100 as Furman beat Newberry 149-95.

Reaching the 100 mark was not easy. Selvy's last six points came in the final 30 seconds, and his final basket was a desperation heave from the top of the key at the far end of the court, some 70 feet away, that just beat the buzzer. "It was my night," said Selvy. "That ball went right through the basket and hit nothing but net. It was one of those shots where more luck than skill was involved. But when a player scores one hundred points, there has to be plenty of both."

Selvy went on to play nine seasons of pro ball for seven teams, averaging 10.8 points per game. He twice reached the NBA Finals with the Los Angeles Lakers.

Did You Know? Selvy almost broke the Boston Celtics' streak of eight straight NBA titles from 1958–59 through 1965–66, but his shot that would have given the Lakers the victory at the end of Game 7 of the 1962 NBA finals bounced off the rim. Instead the Celtics won that game in overtime to keep their streak alive.

NCAA Division I All-Time Scorers

Player, School	Final Year	Points
Pete Maravich, Louisiana State	1970	3,667
Freeman Williams, Portland State	1978	3,249
Lionel Simmons, La Salle	1990	3,217
Alphonso Ford, Mississippi Valley	1993	3,165
Harry Kelly, Texas Southern	1983	3,066
Hersey Hawkins, Bradley	1988	3,008
Oscar Robertson, Cincinnati	1960	2,973
Danny Manning, Kansas	1988	2,951
Alfredrick Hughes, Loyola (Ill.)	1985	2,914
Elvin Hayes, Houston	1968	2,884
Larry Bird, Indiana State	1979	2,850
Otis Birdsong, Houston	1977	2,832
Kevin Bradshaw, U.S. International	1991	2,804
Allan Houston, Tennessee	1993	2,801
Hank Gathers, Loyola Marymount	1990	2,723
Reggie Lewis, Northeastern	1987	2,708
Daren Queenan, Lehigh	1988	2,703
Byron Larkin, Xavier (OH)	1988	2,696
David Robinson, Navy	1987	2,669
Wayman Tisdale, Oklahoma	1985	2,661

Division I Scoring Leaders

Player, College	G	Final Year	Total Pts.	Avg.
Pete Maravich, Louisiana State	83	1968	3667	44.2
Austin Carr, Notre Dame	74	1971	2560	34.6
Oscar Robertson, Cincinnati	66	1960	2973	33.8
Calvin Murphy, Niagara	77	1970	2548	33.1
Dwight Lamar, Southwestern La.	57	1973	1862	32.7
Frank Selvy, Furman	78	1954	2538	32.5
Rick Mount, Purdue	72	1970	2323	32.3
Darrell Floyd, Furman	71	1956	2281	32.1
Nick Werkman, Seton Hall	71	1964	2273	32.0
Willie Humes, Idaho State	48	1971	1510	31.5

SCORING LEADERS, YEAR BY YEAR

Only two players have won as many as three scoring titles in their college careers—Oscar Robertson, Cincinnati, 1958–60, and Pete Maravich, Louisiana State, 1968–70.

Division I Career Scoring Leaders

Season	Player, School	Avg.
1947–48	Murray Wier, Iowa	21.0
1948–49	Tony Lavelli, Yale	22.4
1949–50	Paul Arizin, Villanova	25.3
1950–51	Bill Mlkvy, Temple	29.2
1951–52	Clyde Lovellette, Kansas	28.4
1952–53	Frank Selvy, Furman	29.5
1953–54	Frank Selvy, Furman	41.7
1954–55	Darrell Floyd, Furman	35.9
1955–56	Darrell Floyd, Furman	33.8
1956–57	Grady Wallace, South Carolina	31.2
1957–58	Oscar Robertson, Cincinnati	35.1
1958–59	Oscar Robertson, Cincinnati	32.6
1959–60	Oscar Robertson, Cincinnati	33.7

Division I Career Scoring Leaders (continued)

Season	Player, School	Avg.
1960–61	Frank Burgess, Gonzaga	32.4
1961–62	Billy McGill, Utah	38.8
1962–63	Nick Werkman, Seton Hall	29.5
1963–64	Howard Komives, Bowling Green	36.7
1964–65	Rick Barry, Miami (Fla.)	37.4
1965–66	Dave Schellhase, Purdue	32.5
1966–67	Jimmy Walker, Providence	30.4
1967–68	Pete Maravich, Louisiana State	43.8
1968–69	Pete Maravich, Louisiana State	44.2
1969–70	Pete Maravich, Louisiana State	44.5
1970–71	Johnny Neumann, Mississippi	40.1
1971–72	Dwight Lamar, Southwestern Louisiana	36.3
1972–73	William Averitt, Pepperdine	33.9
1973–74	Larry Fogle, Canisius	33.4
1974–75	Bob McCurdy, Richmond	32.9
1975–76	Marshall Rodgers, Texas–Pan American	36.8
1976–77	Freeman Williams, Portland State	38.8
1977–78	Freeman Williams, Portland State	35.9
1978–79	Lawrence Butler, Idaho State	30.1
1979–80	Tony Murphy, Southern–Birmingham	32.1
1980–81	Zam Fredrick, South Carolina	28.9
1981–82	Harry Kelly, Texas Southern	29.7
1982–83	Harry Kelly, Texas Southern	28.8
1983–84	Joe Jakubick, Akron	30.1
1984–85	Xavier McDaniel, Wichita State	27.2
1985–86	Terrance Bailey, Wagner	29.4
1986–87	Kevin Houston, Army	32.9
1987–88	Hersey Hawkins, Bradley	36.3
1988–89	Hank Gathers, Loyola Marymount	32.7
1989–90	Bo Kimble, Loyola Marymount	35.3
1990–91	Kevin Bradshaw, U.S. International	37.6
1991–92	Brett Roberts, Morehead State	28.1
1992–93	Greg Guy, Texas–Pan American	29.3
1993–94	Glenn Robinson, Purdue	30.3
1994–95	Kurt Thomas, Texas Christian	28.9
1995–96	Kevin Granger, Texas Southern	27.0
1996–97	Charles Jones, Long Island U.	30.1

Oscar Robertson: The Big O

Until Michael Jordan came along, Oscar Robertson was generally regarded as the best all-around basketball player in the history of the game, certainly the best noncenter. Many old-timers still regard Robertson as Number One.

At 6' 5" and 220 pounds, Robertson could do it all. He could shoot from outside or post up his man near the basket and score inside. He had the quickness and agility to drive to the hoop past any defender. He could pass and dribble as well as anyone and was a leading rebounder as well. "Am I the greatest?" said Robertson. "I think I could have played against anybody and played very well against anybody. Look at my record."

Robertson led Crispus Attucks High School in Indianapolis to two state championships and was voted Indiana's "Mr. Basketball" as a senior. Robertson then led the nation in scoring three years in a row at Ohio State, averaging 35.1, 32.2 and 33.7 points per game in his three varsity seasons. He was a unanimous first-team All-American all three years and the college basketball player of the year each time. He led Cincinnati to the NCAA Final Four in 1958–59 and 1959–60, the Bearcats losing to California in the national semifinals both times.

Robertson then served as co-captain with Jerry West of the 1960 U.S. Olympic team that won the gold medal in Rome, leading the team with 17 points per game. Many consider that the greatest amateur basketball team ever assembled, because in addition to Robertson and West, it also included Hall of Famers Jerry Lucas and Walt Bellamy and several players who became solid pros like Adrian Smith, Darrall Imhoff, Terry Dischinger, and Bob Boozer.

A territorial draft choice of the Cincinnati Royals, Robertson became one of the NBA's brightest stars. In 1961–62 he averaged 30.8 points, 12.5 rebounds, and 11.4 assists per game—a triple-double long before the term even was invented. No other player has ever matched that feat.

Robertson spent 10 seasons with Cincinnati before being traded to Milwaukee and joining a young Kareem Abdul-Jabbar to lead the Bucks to the 1970–71 NBA championship. An All-Star for 12 of his 14 NBA seasons, Robertson retired as the NBA's all-time assists leader (since surpassed by John Stockton and Magic Johnson) and the top scoring guard of all time. He was the league's MVP in 1963–64 and one of only four guards (with Johnson, Michael Jordan, and Bob Cousy) to win the honor.

"There were a lot of players who were just as big as I was," said Robertson, "but I could handle the ball, dribble the ball, make the passes. And at the end of the game I wanted the ball, because I felt I was better able to get us a shot than anyone else."

Others may have been better at one part of the game, but for the all-around package, Robertson was unmatched. "Oscar is without a doubt the all-time everything basketball player," said backcourt rival Dave Bing. "His tremendous offensive ability has overshadowed his great defensive skills." Added Lucas, a teammate with the Cincinnati Royals as well as the 1960 Olympic team, "He obviously was unbelievable, way ahead of his time. There is no more complete player than Oscar."

Tom Gola (left), holds his trophy after being named the National College Player of the Year by the Philadelphia Writers Association. Gola stands with college coach Ken Loeffler and professional star Neil Johnston.

Did You Know? Besides his triple-double season of 1961–62, Robertson missed doing it again in two other seasons by less than one rebound per game, and in two more seasons by less than one assist per game.

Rebounding

Most Rebounds in a Game: 51 by Bill Chambers, William & Mary vs. Virginia, February 14, 1953.

Most Rebounds in a Season: 734 by Walter Dukes, Seton Hall, 1952–53.

Most Rebounds in a Career: 2,201 by Tom Gola, La Salle, 1953–55.

Most Rebounds Per Game in a Season: 25.6 by Charlie Slack, Marshall, 1954–55.

Most Rebounds Per Game in a Career: 22.7 by Artis Gilmore, Jacksonville, 1970–71.

Tom Gola: The Philly Phenom

One look at Tom Gola and you'd never suspect he grabbed more rebounds than any other player in college basketball history. He was hardly imposing physically, at least compared to some of the giants who have played the game. Gola, who played for La Salle College in Philadelphia from 1951–52 through 1954–55, stood 6' 6" and played at 205 pounds—figures that would be a drop under the average for an NBA player today.

Gola was a well-rounded player who dribbled well and shot from outside in addition to mixing it up under the boards. His skills enabled him to play any position on the court depending on where he was needed the most—center, forward, or guard. He was one of most celebrated basketball players in Philadelphia's rich history in the sport, starring at La Salle High School before staying home to attend La Salle College, a commuter school with an enrollment of less than 1,000 whose gymnasium was located beneath the high school. His college coach, Hall of Fame member Ken Loeffler, built his team around Gola even when he was just a freshman. "He can do everything and do it well," said Loeffler. "I have never seen one player control a game by himself as well as Gola does." He called his star "Mr. All-Around."

Gola was a starter all four years at La Salle and led his school to the NIT championship as a freshman and the NCAA championship as a junior. In his senior year, La Salle reached the NCAA finals once again but lost to a University of San Francisco team that included Bill Russell and K. C. Jones.

Gola finished his 118-game college career with 2,462 points and 2,201 rebounds, and he remains the leading rebounder in NCAA history. In Gola's four years, La Salle's combined record was 102-19.

He went on to play 10 productive seasons in the NBA, compiling career averages of 11.3 points and 8.0 rebounds per game. He averaged in double figures in scoring seven times and rebounding three times.

Did You Know? Philadelphia public address announcer Dave Zinkoff created a special call for Gola's baskets, describing each as a "Gola goal."

Assists

Most Assists in a Game: 22 by Tony Fairley, Baptist vs. Armstrong State, February 9, 1987; by Avery Johnson, Southern vs. Texas Southern, January 25, 1988; and by Sherman Douglas, Syracuse vs. Providence, January 28, 1989.

Most Assists in a Season: 406 by Mark Wade, UNLV, 1986–87.

Most Assists Per Game in a Season: 13.3 by Avery Johnson, Southern, 1987–88.

Most Assists in a Career: 1,076 by Bobby Hurley, Duke, 1990–93.

Most Assists Per Game in a Career: 8.91 by Avery Johnson, Southern, 1985–88.

Bobby Hurley: No Passing Fancy

As the son of a celebrated high school coach in Jersey City, New Jersey, Bobby Hurley learned the fundamentals of basketball at an early age. And one of those fundamentals is always take good care of the ball. Fancy passes are nice, but not at the risk of turning the ball over. As Red Auerbach likes to say, the best pass is one that is caught by the receiver.

Hurley led St. Anthony's High School, coached by his father, Bobby Hurley, Sr., to a 32-0 record in his senior year and the team finished No. 1 in *USA Today*'s national rankings. Hurley was the team's playmaker, and among the teammates to whom he fed the ball was Terry Dehere, now with the NBA's Los Angeles Clippers.

Heavily recruited by schools throughout the country even though he was only six feet tall, Hurley decided to attend Duke. He stepped right in as a starter and led the Blue Devils to national prominence, feeding the ball to such teammates as Grant Hill, Christian Laettner, Antonio Lang, and Cherokee Parks.

Bobby Hurley led the Blue Devils to three NCAA championship finals during his four-year career at Duke University.

Hurley excelled in running both the fast break and the half-court offense as he helped Duke make three consecutive trips to the NCAA championship game, winning the title in 1990–91 and 1991–92. Hurley was named the Most Outstanding Player at the 1992 Final Four. He posted 27 point-and-assist double-doubles in his 140-game career and finished with averages of 12.4 points and 7.7 assists per game. Hurley's 1,076 career assists are the most in NCAA history, and his 145 assists are the most in the history of the NCAA tournament.

After his junior year, Hurley was a member of an eight man developmental team of collegians that practiced and scrimmaged against the original Dream Team to help it get ready for the 1992 Olympics in Barcelona. He made a good impression going up against NBA guards Magic Johnson and John Stockton, running the team effectively and showing quickness, durability, and decision-making that impressed NBA scouts. Following his senior year he was drafted number one by the Sacramento Kings, the seventh overall pick of the 1993 NBA Draft.

A bright pro career seemed to be in his future, but early in his rookie NBA season, Hurley was nearly killed when a car ran into the vehicle he was driving as he headed home after a game. Hurley was thrown into a roadside ditch and his many injuries included a detached trachea, multiple broken ribs, and a fractured left shoulder. He spent eight days in intensive care, then underwent lengthy rehabilitation before rejoining the Kings for the 1994–95 season.

For most of the past three years, Hurley has struggled to regain the form he showed in college and in his first month as a pro, but he has never given up. He spent most of his time on the bench as a reserve behind point guards Spud Webb and Tyus Edney, but played well late in the 1996–97 season and showed signs of living up to the projections made for him when he left Duke.

Hurley's determination and dedication in working to come back from the injuries he suffered in his accident won the admiration of teammates and fans. He is a national spokesman for the U.S. Department of Transportation for seatbelt safety and has made public service announcements urging everyone to wear seatbelts. He was not wearing his seatbelt at the time of his accident and blames that mistake for the severity of his injuries.

Steals

Most Steals in a Game: 13 by Mookie Blaylock, twice, Oklahoma vs. Centenary, December 12, 1987, and vs. Loyola Marymount, December 17, 1988.

Most Steals in a Season: 150 by Mookie Blaylock, Oklahoma, 1987–88.

Most Steals Per Game in a Season: 4.96 by Darron Brittman, Chicago State, 1985–86.

Most Steals in a Career: 376 by Eric Murdock, Providence, 1988–91.

Most Steals Per Game in a Career: 3.8 by Mookie Blaylock, Oklahoma, 1988–89.

Mookie Blaylock: The Secretary of Defense

In two years at Oklahoma, Daron Oshay "Mookie" Blaylock proved he could do it at both ends of the court. Blaylock averaged 18.2 points, 4.8 assists, and 3.7 rebounds per game, but what drew national attention was his steals average of 3.8 per game—the highest in NCAA history.

A 6' 1" guard with quick feet and even quicker hands, Blaylock played two seasons of junior college ball at Midland before moving on to Oklahoma. In his first year with the Sooners he averaged 16.4 points and 5.9 assists per game and also made 150 steals to set an NCAA record. In 1988-89 he became the first player in college history to record back-to-back seasons of 200 assists and 100 steals, and he raised his scoring average to 20 points per game.

On December 12, 1987, Blaylock set an NCAA record by making 13 steals in a game against Centenary. Just over one year later, as if to prove it was no fluke, he matched his mark with another lucky 13 against Loyola Marymount.

Blaylock was selected by New Jersey on the first round of the 1989 NBA Draft, the twelfth player taken. He had three good seasons with the Nets, but after New Jersey drafted Kenny Anderson his days were numbered. In 1992, he was traded to Atlanta, and that is where he blossomed into an All-Star.

In five seasons with the Hawks, Blaylock has gotten at least 200 steals every season and in 1996-97 he led the league at 2.72 steals per game. His offensive game also has flourished as he notched a career-high 17.4 points per game in 1996-97 and ranked second in the NBA with 221 three-point field goals.

Did You Know? Mookie Blaylock holds the Atlanta Hawks team records for assists in a game, 23, and steals in a game, 9.

Blocked Shots

Most Blocked Shots in a Game: 14 by David Robinson, Navy vs. NC-Wilmington, January 4, 1986, and by Shawn Bradley, Brigham Young vs. Eastern Kentucky, December 7, 1990.

Most Blocked Shots in a Season: 207 by David Robinson, Navy, 1985–86.

Most Blocked Shots Per Game in a Season: 5.91 by David Robinson, Navy, 1985–86.

Most Blocked Shots in a Career: 453 by Alonzo Mourning, Georgetown, 1989–92.

Most Blocked Shots Per Game in a Career: 5.24 by David Robinson, Navy, 1986–87.

David Robinson: The Shotblocking Admiral

David Robinson stood 6' 6" and had played only one year of high school basketball before entering the United States Naval Academy. Then he started growing. And growing. And growing. When he was finished, he topped out at 7' 1" and 250 pounds. Combine that size with the all-around skills he had developed as a smaller player, and the result was one of the most versatile and talented centers of all time.

Fast, strong, and agile, he was the best thing that ever happened to Navy basketball, a devastating force at both ends of the court. After a freshman season of adjustment to his new stature, Robinson blossomed as a sophomore and averaged 23.6 points and 11.6 rebounds per game, the first of three successive 20-10 seasons.

As a junior he led the nation in rebounding at 13.0 per game and set an NCAA Division I record by averaging 5.91 blocks per game. He blocked 14 shots in a single game to set an NCAA record, and his 207 blocks for the season set another record. Having established all those defensive marks as a junior, he boosted his offense as a senior to 28.2 points per game. That plus 11.8 rebounds and 4.5 blocks earned him unanimous Player of the Year honors.

David Robinson blocks a shot during a NCAA tournament game against Cleveland State.

The San Antonio Spurs, with the first pick in the NBA Draft, faced a dilemma. Robinson obviously was a unique player, but as a Navy graduate he would be required to spend at least two and possibly four years in military service. Should they draft him and wait, hoping his skills did not lessen in the meantime, or should they take someone else who could help them right away?

The Spurs took Robinson, and he proved to be worth the wait. He spent two years in the Navy, where he was stationed at a submarine base, and managed to get time off to compete in the 1988 Olympics in Korea. That would be the first of three consecutive Olympic appearances for Robinson—he's the only male basketball player to represent the United States in three Olympics.

When he finally joined the Spurs in 1989–90 he earned Rookie of the Year honors by averaging 24.3 points, 12.0 rebounds and 3.89 blocks and shooting .531 from the field. San Antonio had posted a 21-61 record in 1988–89, but in Robinson's rookie year the Spurs went 56-26 and captured the Midwest Division title. The 35-game improvement marked the greatest single-season turnaround in NBA history.

In his first seven NBA seasons, he won (in addition to the Rookie of the Year award) a rebounding title, a scoring crown, a Most Valuable Player award, a Defensive Player of the Year award, seven All-Star selections, four selections to the All-NBA First Team, and four selections to the NBA All-Defensive First Team. Although Robinson missed most of the 1996–97 season due to two injuries, a strained back and a broken foot, his eighth year wasn't a total loss—he was honored as one of the NBA's "50 Greatest Players of All Time," as chosen by a panel of basketball experts.

Robinson has also become one of the most beloved members of the San Antonio community. A devout Christian, he has established a foundation to support programs that address the physical and spiritual needs of the family and is extremely active in civic and charitable affairs. He also is a talented musician and an avid computer buff.

Did You Know? David Robinson scored 1,320 on his SAT College Board exam, out of a possible 1,600.

Division II Records

Most Points in a Game: 113 by Bevo Francis, Rio Grande vs. Hillsdale, February 4, 1954.

Most Points Per Game in a Season: 46.5 by Bevo Francis, Hillsdale, 1953–54.

Most Points in a Career: 4,045 by Travis Grant, Kentucky State, 1969–72.

Most Points Per Game in a Career: 33.4 by Travis Grant, Kentucky State, 1969–72.

Most Rebounds Per Game in a Season: 29.5 by Tom Hart, Middlebury, 1954–55 and 1956.

Most Rebounds Per Game in a Career: 27.6 by Tom Hart, Middlebury, 1953–56.

Most Assists in a Season: 400 by Steve Ray, Bridgeport, 1988–89.

Most Assists Per Game in a Season: 12.5 by Steve Ray, Bridgeport, 1988–89.

Most Assists in a Career: 1,044 by Demetri Beekman, Assumption, 1990–93.

Most Assists Per Game in a Career: 12.1 by Steve Ray, Bridgeport, 1989–90.

Highest Field Goal Percentage in a Season: .752 by Todd Linder, Tampa, 1986–87.

Highest Field Goal Percentage in a Career: .708 by Todd Linder, Tampa, 1984–87.

Highest Free Throw Percentage in a Season: .944 by Billy Newton, Morgan State, 1975–76 and by Kent Andrews, McNeese State, 1967–68.

Highest Free Throw Percentage in a Career: .916 by Kent Andrews, McNeese State, 1967–69.

Division III Records

Most Points in a Game: 69 by Steve Diekman, Grinnell vs. Simpson, 1995.

Most Points Per Game in a Season: 37.3 by Steve Diekman, Grinnell, 1994–95.

Most Points in a Career: 2,940 by Andre Foreman, Salisbury State, 1989–92.

Most Points Per Game in a Career: 32.8 by Dwain Govan, Bishop, 1974–75.

Most Rebounds Per Game in a Season: 20.0 by Joe Manley, Bowie State, 1975–76.

Most Rebounds Per Game in a Career: 17.4 by Larry Parker, Plattsburgh State, 1975–78.

Most Assists in a Season: 391 by Robert James, Kean, 1988–89.

Most Assists Per Game in a Season: 13.5 by Robert James, Kean, 1988–89.

Most Assists Per Game in a Career: 8.1 by Steve Artis, Christopher Newport, 1990–93.

Highest Field Goal Percentage in a Season: .766 by Travis Weiss, St. John's (Minnesota), 1993–94.

Highest Field Goal Percentage in a Career: .953 by Andy Enfield, Johns Hopkins, 1991.

SMALL COLLEGE STANDOUTS

Some of basketball's brightest stars have come from the small college ranks, including Hall of Famers like Walt Frazier (Southern Illinois), Joe Fulks (Murray State), Harry Gallatin (Northeast Missouri), George Gervin (Eastern Michigan), Sam Jones (North Carolina Central), Vern Mikkelsen (Hamline), Earl Monroe (Winston-Salem State), and Willis Reed (Grambling).

It's also worth noting that the coaches of the teams with the two best records in the NBA in 1996–97, Phil Jackson of the Chicago Bulls and Jerry Sloan of the Utah Jazz, came from small colleges and had fine NBA careers before becoming successful coaches. Jackson attended North Dakota while Sloan went to Evansville.

Earl "The Pearl" Monroe spent his collegiate years at Winston-Salem State. Monroe went on to have an outstanding career in the NBA.

Small College Stars

Player, College, 1996–97 NBA Team

Vin Baker, Hartford, Milwaukee Bucks
Mario Elie, American International, Houston Rockets
Derek Fisher, Arkansas-Little Rock, Los Angeles Lakers
Lindsay Hunter, Jackson State, Detroit Pistons
Jerome Kersey, Longwood, Los Angeles Lakers
Rick Mahorn, Hampton Institute, Detroit Pistons
Charles Oakley, Virginia Union, New York Knicks
Scottie Pippen, Central Arkansas, Chicago Bulls
Terry Porter, Wisconsin-Stevens Point, Minnesota Timberwolves
Dennis Rodman, Southeastern Oklahoma, Chicago Bulls
Rik Smits, Marist, Indiana Pacers
Sedale Threatt, West Virginia Tech, Houston Rockets

WINNINGEST COLLEGE COACHES OF ALL TIME

The 10 Winningest Coaches

Coach	Wins
Dean Smith	879
Adolph Rupp	876
Henry Iba	767
Ed Diddle	759
Phog Allen	746
Ray Meyer	724
Bob Knight	698
Don Haskins	691
Norm Stewart	691
Ralph Miller	674

Top Winners by Percentage

Coach	Record	Pct.
Clair Bee (Rider, Long Island U.)	412- 87	.826
Adolph Rupp (Kentucky)	876-190	.822
Jerry Tarkanian (Long Beach State, UNLV, Fresno State)	673-146	.822
John Wooden (Indiana State, UCLA)	664-162	.804
Dean Smith (North Carolina)	879-254	.776

Only three coaches in history have won NCAA, NIT, and Olympic titles. Indiana head coach Bob Knight won three NCAA championships ('76, '81, '87), the NIT in 1979 and the Olympic gold medal in 1984. Dean Smith's Tar Heels won two NCAA titles ('82, '93), the NIT in 1971, and the Olympic gold medal in 1976. Pete Newell won the NCAA title in 1959 at California, the NIT in 1949 at San Francisco, and the U.S. Olympic gold medal in 1960.

TEAM RECORDS FOR DIVISION I COMPETITION

Regular Season

Most Points in a Game: 186 by Loyola Marymount vs. U.S. International, January 5, 1991.

Fewest Points in a Game: 6 by Temple in an 11-6 loss to Tennessee on December 15, 1973, and by Arkansas State in a 75-6 loss to Kentucky on January 8, 1945.

Most Points Per Game in a Season: 122.4 by Loyola Marymount, 1989–90.

Fewest Points Per Game Allowed in a Season (since 1938): 25.7 by Oklahoma State, 1938–39.

NCAA Tournament

Most Points in a Game: 149 by Loyola Marymount vs. Michigan, 1990.

Fewest Points in a Game: 20 by North Carolina in a 26-20 loss to Pittsburgh, 1941.

Dean Smith has more wins than any other coach in college history. Here he's shown cutting down the net after his Tar Heels defeated Georgetown in the national championship game in 1982.

Most Points by Two Teams in a Game: 264 by Loyola Marymount (149) vs. Michigan (115), 1990.

Most Points Per Game in One Tournament: 105.8 by Loyola Marymount, 1990.

WOMEN'S BASKETBALL

Women's basketball has grown faster in both participation and popularity than any other area of the sport in the past two decades.

Nearly one-half million girls play interscholastic high school basketball, and thousands more compete in intramural hoops. Women's college basketball has hit the big time, with the NCAA Women's Final Four an annual sellout that is televised nationally to an ever-growing audience. More than 5.2 million fans attended women's college basketball games in 1995–96 (not counting doubleheaders with men's teams), the last year for which statistics were available.

The USA Basketball Women's National Team was an unprecedented success competitively as well as with fans and sponsors in 1995–96. Bringing together the best American basketball players for a year of training and exhibitions, the team won games and fans wherever it went, beating every opponent on a 52-game global exhibition tour. The team capped its run by winning a gold medal at the Olympic Games in Atlanta and capturing the public's imagination, drawing more than 30,000 fans to each of its games at the Georgia Dome.

This spectacular growth led to the creation of not one but two women's professional leagues which began play in the United States in 1996 and 1997. Other pro leagues had been tried in the past but had never lasted very long, and the best American college stars had been forced to play in Europe, Asia, or South America if they wanted to compete professionally. Not anymore.

The American Basketball League averaged crowds nearly 20 percent above its preseason projection of 3,000 per game in its inaugural season in the winter of 1996–97, as eight teams competed in a 40-game schedule. Months later, the Women's NBA, backed by the money and marketing might of the National Basketball Association, launched its first season with eight teams playing 32-game schedules in the summer of 1997. Both leagues boasted big-name sponsors and national television coverage, something that had never been achieved by earlier pro leagues and should assure the survival and growth of women's professional basketball in the United States.

More and more people are discovering the beauty and excitement of women's basketball, where the game is basically played below the rim (dunks are extremely rare at even the highest levels of women's basketball). Lacking above the rim sky-hooks and high-flying jams, female basketball players make up for it by placing a premium on fundamentals and smart play. When it comes to precise passing, controlled dribbling, boxing out under the boards, and well-executed plays, the women do it as well as the men, if not better.

The following is a look at women's basketball at the collegiate, Olympic, and professional levels (the high school game is covered in chapter 5). All statistics and records on the college game are courtesy of the NCAA and are complete through the 1995–96 season, the latest for which such information is available. ABL records are courtesy of the American Basketball League; stats for the inaugural season of the WNBA were not available at publication time.

COLLEGE BASKETBALL

The first known women's basketball game between two colleges took place on April 4, 1896, between Stanford and the University of California. No men were permitted to attend, and when two men had to enter the gym to prop up a basket, it was reported that "the Berkeley team screamed and hid in a corner." Once the basket was fixed and the men left the building, the game continued and Stanford posted a 2-1 victory.

Scoring in the women's game has come a long way since then. Long Beach State set an NCAA record by beating San Jose

State 149-69 in 1987, and four years later Virginia and North Carolina State set another record with a combined 243 points in Virginia's 123-120 triple overtime victory.

Scoring isn't the only thing that has changed in women's basketball. The rules and administration of the sport have undergone volatile changes over the years.

In 1899, a committee led by Senda Berenson Abbott of Smith College, who is recognized as the "Mother of Women's Basketball," adopted rules calling for the court to be divided into three sections, with players restricted to those sections. Other rules were also used, but by the 1920s the three-section game was the accepted standard, with the number of players between five and ten.

The birth of the WNBA has allowed women's professional basketball to enter into the national spotlight.

In the 1930s the court was divided into two parts, and six players on a team, three guards and three forwards, became the norm. That's the way it remained until the 1960s, when two of the six players were designated as "rovers" and permitted to move between sections. In 1969 this was taken a major step further with experimental use of five-player teams playing a full-court game—just like the men. In 1971 it became the official standard for women's play, although what became known as "six-girl basketball" continued in some areas into the early 1990s.

This evolution in rules is reflected in the administration of women's basketball in the United States. By 1920, women's basketball was being played all around the world, but in the United States it was held back on the intercollegiate level because some thought such athletic competition was not femi-

Women's basketball has come a long way since the early 1900s. Players no longer wear skirts, and it would be difficult to find a referee wearing a coat and hat.

nine. The Amateur Athletic Union stepped into this void and in 1926 organized the first National Women's Basketball Championship. By 1929 this became an annual event. The famed athlete Babe Didrikson, playing for a team called the Golden Cyclones, averaged over 20 points per game to lead her team to the 1931 AAU title.

Women's collegiate basketball finally began to move forward in the 1950s and 1960s thanks to two small schools, Wayland College of Plainview, Texas, and the Nashville Business College in Tennessee. During their heyday Nashville had players recognized as All-Americans 76 times, Wayland 60 times, and the two schools won every National AAU title from 1956 through 1969.

Scholarships and Plane Rides

Wayland, coached by Harley Redin, offered full scholarships to women basketball players and, with the support of a local businessman, Claude Hutcherson, flew its team to all road games on private airplanes. The Hutcherson Flying Queens, as they became known, won 131 consecutive games. In the National AAU Tournament they finished first 10 times and second 9 times, compiling a 431-66 record in 18 seasons.

Wayland's 131-game streak came to an end at the 1958 AAU title game when it was beaten by the Nashville Business College 46-42. Nashville Business College, coached by John Head, won 96 games in a row and captured 11 AAU championships, including 8 in a row from 1962 through 1969.

The greatest player of this era was Nera White, a versatile athlete who was elected to the Hall of Fame in 1962. White was a brilliant shooter with great range who also could run and jump like the best of the men. She starred for the Nashville Business College and was named the AAU Tournament's Most

Valuable Player 10 times and an All-American 15 years in a row. In 1957 she led the United States to the World Basketball Championship in Brazil, winning MVP honors there as well.

In 1969, the first National Intercollegiate Women's Basketball Tournament was held at West Chester State College and won by Immaculata, signaling the start of a new era in women's college basketball. Two years later the Association of Intercollegeiate Athletics for Women was formed. From 1971 through 1982, when it gave way to the NCAA, the AIAW would be the governing body for women's intercollegiate sports. Poorly funded and understaffed, the AIAW organized and promoted championships in basketball and other sports for women at a time when the NCAA shunned such an effort, fearing it would take away money from the lucrative men's basketball and football programs.

After receiving the MVP award during the 1957 World Basketball Championships, Nera White was selected as the "best woman player in the world."

A GREAT PASS BY CONGRESS

Women's sports got a major boost with the passage of Title IX of the Educational Amendments of 1972, which sought to promote gender equity and stated, "No person in the U.S. shall, on the basis of sex, be excluded from participation in, or denied the benefits of, or be subjected to discrimination under any educational program or activity receiving federal aid." Title IX forced schools to devote greater resources to women's athletic programs, including scholarships, and facilities.

The AIAW stressed the concept of the student-athlete and the importance of women athletes being treated like any other students. Nonscholarship or modest-budget schools like Delta

State, Immaculata, Montclair State, Queens, and Wayland Baptist prospered under the democratic atmosphere fostered by the AIAW. Some of the greatest stars in women's basketball history competed during the AIAW era, including Carol Blazejowski, Nancy Lieberman-Cline, Anne Donovan, Lusia Harris, and Ann Meyers, all members of the Basketball Hall of Fame.

Connecticut's **Rebecca Lobo** and **Pam Weber** cut down the net after the Huskies defeated Virginia 67-63 in the 1995 East Regional championship.

The NCAA replaced the AIAW as basketball's governing body in 1982, and conducted its first National Basketball Championship. The Final Four has grown into one of the major events on the annual sports calendar.

It's Unbelievable, Baby!

In 1994, North Carolina beat Louisiana Tech for the title 60-59 on a last-second shot by Charlotte Smith, while in 1995 Connecticut beat Tennessee 70-64 to complete an unbeaten season, with stars Rebecca Lobo, Jennifer Rizzotti, and Kara Wolters. A capacity crowd of 23,291 filled the Charlotte Coliseum in 1996 when Tennessee, coached by Pat Head Summitt, beat Georgia 83-65. The Tennessee Vols repeated as champions in 1997 by beating Old Dominion 68-59 for a record fifth NCAA title. Nationally televised by CBS, the Final Four has drawn increasing ratings each year, reflecting the widening popularity of the women's game.

Regular season games are drawing increasing attention as well—a crowd of 24,563 (including 23,912 paid), the most ever to attend a women's game, saw Texas defeat Tennessee 97-78 on December 9, 1987 at Thompson-Boling Arena in Knoxville, Tennessee.

CHAMPIONSHIPS

Following are the year-by-year champions of major women's college basketball.

AIAW Championships

Season	Championship Game
1971–72	Immaculata 52, West Chester 48
1972–73	Immaculata 59, Queens (N.Y.) 52
1973–74	Immaculata 68, Mississippi Col. 53
1974–75	Delta State 90, Immaculata 81
1975–76	Delta State 69, Immaculata 4
1976–77	Delta State 68, Louisiana State 55
1977–78	UCLA 90, Maryland 74
1978–79	Old Dominion 75, Louisiana Tech 65
1979–80	Old Dominion 68, Tennessee 53
1980–81	Louisiana Tech 79, Tennessee 59
1981–82	Rutgers 83, Texas 77

NCAA Division I Finals

Season	Championship Game, MVP
1981–82	Louisiana Tech 76, Cheyney 62—Janice Lawrence, La. Tech
1982–83	Southern Cal. 69, Louisiana Tech 67—Cheryl Miller, Southern Cal.
1983–84	Southern Cal. 72, Tennessee 61—Cheryl Miller, Southern Cal.
1984–85	Old Dominion 70, Georgia 65—Tracy Claxton, Old Dominion
1985–86	Texas 97, Southern Cal 81—Clarissa Davis, Texas
1986–87	Tennessee 67, Louisiana Tech 44—Tonya Edwards, Tennessee

Season	Championship Game, MVP
1987–88	Louisiana Tech 56, Auburn 54, Erica Westbrooks, La. Tech
1988–89	Tennessee 76, Auburn 60, Bridgette Gordon, Tennessee
1989–90	Stanford 88, Auburn 81, Jennifer Azzi, Stanford
1990–91	Tennessee 70, Virginia 67 (OT), Dawn Staley, Virginia
1991–92	Stanford 78, Western Kentucky 62, Molly Goodenbour, Stanford
1992–93	Texas Tech 84, Ohio State 82, Sheryl Swoopes, Texas Tech
1993–94	North Carolina 60, Louisiana Tech 59, Charlotte Smith, North Carolina
1994–95	Connecticut 70, Tennessee 64, Rebecca Lobo, Connecticut
1995–96	Tennessee 83, Georgia 65, Michelle Marciniak, Tenneessee
1996–97	Tennessee 68, Old Dominion 59, Chamique Holdsclaw, Tennessee

INDIVIDUAL NCAA RECORDS

Following are NCAA women's basketball records which cover play since 1982, when the NCAA replaced the AIAW as the sport's governing body. All records are complete through the 1995–96 season, and all are for Division I except where indicated.

At the end are selected AIAW career records.

Most Points in a Game: 60 by Cindy Brown, Long Beach State vs. San Jose State, February 16, 1987.

Most Points, Division II, in a Game: 67 by Jackie Givens, Fort Valley State, vs. Knoxville, February 22, 1991.

Most Points, Division III, in a Game: 61 by Ann Gilbert, Oberlin vs. Allegheny, February 6, 1991.

Most Points in a Season: 974 by Cindy Brown, Long Beach State, 1986–87.

Most Points, Division II, in a Season: 1,075 by Jackie Givens, Fort Valley State, 1990–91.

Most Points, Division III, in a Season: 891 by Jeannie Demers, Buena Vista, 1986–87.

Most Points Per Game in a Season: 33.6 by Patricia Hoskins, Mississippi Valley, 1988–89.

Most Points Per Game, Division II, in a Season: 38.4 by Jackie Givens, Fort Valley State, 1990–91.

Most Points Per Game, Division III, in a Season: 34.3 by Jeannie Demers, Buena Vista, 1986–87.

Most Points in a Career: 3,122 by Patricia Hoskins, Mississippi Valley, 1985–89.

Most Points, Division II, in a Career: 2,810 by Dina Kangas, Minn.-Duluth, 1988–91.

Cheryl Miller led the USC Trojans to back-to-back NCAA titles in 1983 and 1984.

Most Points, Division III, in a Career: 3,171 by Jeannie Demers, Buena Vista, 1984–87.

Most Points Per Game in a Career: 28.4 by Patricia Hoskins, Mississippi Valley, 1985–89.

Most Points Per Game, Division II, in a Career: 28.3 by Paulette King, Florida Tech, 1992–93.

Most Points Per Game, Division III, in a Career: 30.2 by Jeannie Demers, Buena Vista, 1984–87.

Highest Field Goal Percentage in a Season: .721 (199-for-276) by Daneka Knowles, Southeastern Louisiana, 1995–96.

Highest Field Goal Percentage in a Career: .681 (578-for-849) by Daneka Knowles, Southeastern Louisiana, 1992–96.

Most Consecutive Field Goals in a Game: 17 by Dorinda Lindstron, Santa Clara vs. Fresno State, November 30, 1986.

Most Consecutive Field Goals in a Season: 23 by Renay Adams, Tennessee Tech, 1990–91, by Mary Ostrowski, Tennessee, 1983–84, and by Pam Kelly, Louisiana Tech, 1981–82.

Most Field Goals Made, None Missed, in a Game: 16 by Kelly Mago, Southwest Missouri State vs. Bradley, February 18, 1988.

Most Three-Point Field Goals in a Game: 12 by Cornelia Gayden, LSU vs. Jackson State, February 9, 1995.

Most Consecutive Three-Point Field Goals in a Game: 9 by Susan Smith, Eastern Washington vs. Weber State, February 13, 1988.

Most Three-Point Field Goals in a Season: 126 by Lisa McMullen, Alabama State, 1991.

Most Three-Point Field Goal Attempts in a Season: 390 by Lisa McMullen, Alabama State, 1990–91.

Highest Three-Point Field Goal Percentage in a Season: .575 (50-for-87) by Heather Donlon, Fordham, 1989–90.

Most Consecutive Three-Point Field Goals: 14 by Deana Lansing, Portland, February 10–17, 1996.

Most Consecutive Games with at Least One Three-Point Field Goal in a Season: 32 by Michelle Hughes, Portland State, 1990–91.

Most Consecutive Games with at Least One Three-Point Field Goal: 53 by Sandy Brown, Middle Tennessee State, 1988–89.

Most Free Throws in a Game: 23 by Shaunda Greene, Washington vs. Northern Illinois, November 30, 1991.

Most Free Throw Attempts in a Game: 31 by Renee Daniels, Southeastern Louisiana vs. New Orleans, January 23, 1985.

Most Consecutive Free Throws Made in a Game: 18 by Chris Starr, Nevada vs. San Diego, January 3, 1984, by Holly Jones, Rice vs. UC-Santa Barbara, November 30, 1985, by Beth Shearer, American vs. Lehigh, December 28, 1987, by Wendy Scholtens, Venderbilt vs. Tennessee Tech, January 11, 1989, and by Donna Abbott, West Virginia vs. Northern Illinois, December 29, 1990.

Most Consecutive Free Throws in a Season: 60 by Ginny Doyle, Richmond, 1991–92.

Highest Free Throw Percentage in a Season: .950 (96-for-101) by Ginny Doyle, Richmond, 1991–92.

Most Free Throws in a Career: 907 by Lorri Bauman, Drake, 1981–84.

Most Free Throw Attempts in a Career: 1,173 by Valerie Whiteside, Appalachian State, 1994.

Most Consecutive Free Throws: 66 by Ginny Doyle, Richmond, 1991–92.

Highest Free Throw Percentage in a Career (minimum 250 free throws made): .867 (269-for-307) by Karen Murray, Washington, 1991–94.

Most Rebounds in a Game: 40 by Deborah Temple, Delta State vs. UAB, February 14, 1983.

Most Rebounds in a Season: 534 by Wanda Ford, Drake, 1984–85.

Most Rebounds in a Career: 1,887 by Wanda Ford, Drake, 1983–86.

Most Assists in a Game: 23 by Michelle Burden, Kent vs. Ball State, February 6, 1991.

Most Assists in a Season: 355 by Suzie McConnell, Penn State, 1986–87.

Most Assists in a Career: 1,307 by Suzie McConnell, Penn State, 1984–88.

Most Blocked Shots in a Game: 15 by Amy Lundquist, Loyola Marymount vs. Western Illinois, December 20, 1992.

Most Blocked Shots in a Season: 151 by Michelle Wilson, Texas Southern, 1988-89.

Most Blocked Shots in a Career: 428 by Genia Miller, Cal. St. Fullerton, 1987–91.

Most Steals in a Game: 14 by Stephanie Wine, Marshall vs. Western Carolina, January 23, 1995, by Heidi Caruso, Lafayette vs. Kansas State, December 5, 1992, and by Natalie White, Florida A&M vs. South Alabama, December 13, 1991.

Most Steals in a Season: 191 by Natalie White, Florida A&M, 1994–95.

Most Steals in a Career: 624 by Natalie White, Florida A&M, 1991–95.

TEAM RECORDS

Most Victories in a Season: 35 by Texas, 1981–82, by Louisiana Tech, 1981–82, by Tennessee, 1988-89, and by Connecticut, 1994–95.

Most Defeats in a Season: 28 by Charleston Southern, 1990–91.

Most Consecutive Victories: 54 by Louisiana Tech, December 1, 1980, to January 27, 1982.

Most Consecutive Home Victories: 69 by Tennessee, February 1, 1991, to January 2, 1996.

Most Consecutive Defeats: 58 by Brooklyn, February 7, 1987 to February 22, 1989.

Most Points in a Game: 149 by Long Beach State vs. San Jose State (69), February 16, 1987.

Fewest Points Allowed in a Game: 12 by North Carolina A&T (85) vs. Bennett, November 21, 1990.

Most Points by Both Teams in a Game: 243 by Virginia (123) and North Carolina State (120), 3 OT, January 12, 1991.

Most Points, Division II, in a Game: 148 by Clarion vs. Westminster (Pennsylvania) (62), November 20, 1992.

Most Points, Division III, in a Game: 140 by Plymouth State vs. Hawthorne (41), February 14, 1983, and by Bishop vs. Concordia (Texas) (75), February 21, 1986.

Most Points, Division II, in a Season: 3,357 by Hampton, 1987–88.

Most Points, Division III, in a Season: 3,023 by North Central, 1981–82.

Most Points Per Game in a Season: 96.7 by Providence, 1990–91.

Fewest Points Per Game Allowed in a Season: 51.8 by Mo.–Kansas City, 1990–91.

Highest Field Goal Percentage in a Game (minimum 18 field goals made): .792 (19-for-24) by Arkansas State vs. Memphis, January 15, 1987.

Highest Field Goal Percentage in a Season: .559 (945-for-1,691) by Drake, 1983-84.

Most Three-Point Field Goals in a Game: 17 by South Carolina vs. Western Carolina, January 13, 1994.

Most Three-Point Field Goal Attempts in a Game: 52 by Alabama vs. Duke, March 18, 1995.

Most Consecutive Three-Point Field Goals in a Game: 11 by Texas Christian vs. Lamar, March 3, 1996.

Most Three-Point Field Goals in a Season: 248 by South Carolina, 1993–94.

Most Consecutive Games with at Least One Three-Point Field Goal: 211 by Tennessee Tech, 1989-96 (current into 1996–97).

Most Free Throws in a Game: 51 by Washington vs. Northern Illinois, November 30, 1991 (2 OT).

Most Free Throw Attempts in a Game: 69 by Washington vs. Northern Illinois, November 30, 1991.

Most Consecutive Free Throws in a Season: 48 by Kansas, February 9-16, 1995–96.

Highest Free Throw Percentage in a Season: .798 (479-for-600) by La Salle, 1987–88.

Most Rebounds in a Game: 92 by Pittsburgh vs. George Washington, January 6, 1982.

Most Rebounds in a Season: 1,997 by Texas Southern, 1981–82.

Most Assists in a Game: 43 by Nebraska vs. Howard, December 11, 1992, and by Northwestern State vs. Arkansas Baptist, January 10, 1987.

Most Assists in a Season: 786 by Connecticut, 1994–95.

Most Blocked Shots in a Game: 18 by Loyola Marymount vs. Western Illinois, December 20, 1992, by Rutgers vs. Oklahoma State, December 28, 1991, and by Vanderbilt vs. Tennessee State, December 10, 1991.

Most Blocked Shots in a Season: 250 by Connecticut, 1994–95.

Most Steals in a Game: 38 by Grambling vs. Texas College, December 10, 1987.

Most Steals in a Season: 536 by Kent, 1992–93.

Most Overtime Periods: 4 by Alabama (121) vs. Duke (120), March 18, 1995, by Duke (112) vs. Northern Iowa (106), January

23, 1993, by Texas A&M (101) vs. St. Mary's (Tex.) (95), December 17, 1984, by Indiana State (107) vs. Southwest Missouri State (101), January 28, 1989, by Creighton (117) vs. Loyola, Ill. (108), January 12, 1986, and by Columbia (114) vs. Pennsylvania (111), March 5, 1988.

Most Overtime Games in a Season: 5 by Northwestern State (won 4, lost 1), 1990, and by Ohio State (won 3, lost 2), 1989–90.

Most Consecutive Overtime Games: 3 by Stephen F. Austin (won 2, lost 1), 1993, and by James Madisonn (won 2, lost 1), 1992.

UNBEATEN TEAMS

Only five college teams have posted unbeaten seasons since 1982. Connecticut (35-0, 1995) and Texas (34-0, 1986) did it at the Division I level. North Dakota State (32-0, 1995) accomplished it in Division II, and capital (33-0, 1995) and Wis.–Oshkosh (31-0, 1996) went unbeaten in Division III.

10 Highest Scorers

Player, Team, and Opponent, Points, Date

Cindy Brown, Long Beach State vs. San Jose State, 60, 2/16/87
Lorri Bauman, rake vs. Southwest Missouri State, 58, 1/6/84
Kim Perrot, Southwestern La. vs. Southeastern La., 58, 2/5/90
Patricia Hoskins, Mississippi Valley vs. Southern U., 55, 2/13/89
Patricia Hoskins, Mississippi Valley vs. Alabama State, 55, 2/25/89
Anjinea Hopson, Grambling vs. Jackson State, 54, 2/21/94
Mary Lowry, Baylor vs. Texas, 54, 2/16/94
Wanda Ford, Drake vs. Southwest Missouri State, 54, 2/22/86
Chris Starr, Nevada vs. Cal. St. Sacramento, 53, 2/8/83
Felisha Edwards, Northeast Louisiana vs.Southern Miss., 53, 3/1/91
Sheryl Swoopes, Texas Tech vs. Texas, 53, 3/13/93

NCAA Division I Scoring Leaders

Year	Player, School	Avg.
1981–82	Barbara Kennedy, Clemson	29.3
1982–83	LaTaunya Pollard, Long Beach State	29.3
1983–84	Deborah Temple, Delta State	31.2
1984–85	Anucha Browne, Northwestern	30.5
1985–86	Wanda Ford, Duke	30.6
1986–87	Tresa Spaulding, Brigham Young	28.9
1987–88	LeChandra LeDay, Grambling	30.4
1988–89	Patricia Hoskins, Mississippi Valley	33.6
1989–90	Kim Perrot, Southwestern Louisiana	30.0
1990–91	Jan Jensen, Drake	29.6
1991–92	Andrea Congreaves, Mercer	33.0
1992–93	Andrea Congreaves, Mercer	31.0
1993–94	Kristy Ryan, Cal. St.-Sacramento	28.0
1994–95	Koko Lahanas, Cal. St.-Fullerton	26.8
1995–96	Cindy Blodgett, Maine	27.8
1996–97	Cindy Blodgett, Maine	27.0

CAREER AIAW RECORDS

The following are career records for players who played all or most of their careers before the era of official NCAA women's basketball statistics. Prior to 1981–82, most women's programs were under the auspices of the AIAW.

Most Points: 3,649 by Lynette Woodard, Kansas, 1978–81.

Highest Scoring Average: 31.7 by Carol Blazejowski, Montclair State, 1975–78.

Highest Field Goal Percentage: .692 by Carol Menken Schaudt, Oregon State, 1979-81.

Highest Free Throw Percentage: .847 by Marsha Cowart, E. Tennessee State, 1980–83.

Most Rebounds: 1,999 by Anne Gregory, Fordham, 1977–80.

Highest Rebound Average: 21.5 by Carla Gadsen, Jersey City State, 1981–82.

WOMEN IN THE HALL OF FAME

Since 1984, women have been recognized with basketball's highest honor: induction into the Naismith Memorial Basketball Hall of Fame. Senda Berenson Abbott, one of the sport's founders, and legendary women's coaches Margaret Wade and Bertha Teague were the first women to be inducted to the Hall.

They since have been joined by some of the outstanding women stars of recent years, including Lusia Harris, Cheryl Miller, Carol Blazejowski, Ann Meyers, Ann Donovan, Juliana Semanova, and Denise Curry. Harris is the only woman to have been drafted by an NBA team (New Orleans Jazz, 1985), while Lieberman-Cline played in the USBL, a men's pro summer league, and Meyers attended training camp with the NBA's Indiana Pacers.

Carol Blazejowski: Blazing a Trail

Playing in an era before women's basketball was recognized by the NCAA, Carol Blazejowski was one of the sport's pioneers, winning fans with her skill and competitiveness. Blazejowski proved that girls could put the ball in the basket just like boys.

In four seasons at Montclair (New Jersey) State College, from 1974–75 through 1977–78, Blazejowski scored more points, 3,199, and compiled a higher average, 31.7 points per game, than any other woman in history to that point. A three-time All-American, she was the Converse Women's Player of the Year in 1977 and the first-ever recipient of the Wade Trophy as the Women's Player of the Year in 1978.

Perhaps her finest moment came on March 6, 1977, at New York's Madison Square Garden in a women's basketball doubleheader that drew 12,336 fans and national media attention. Top-ranked Delta State defeated second-ranked Immaculata 79-62 in the featured game of the doubleheader, but it was Blazejowski who stole the show in the opener.

Carol Blazejowski convinced basketball fans in the late 1970s that women are capable of putting the ball through the hoop.

Driving to the basket and hitting jump shots from all over the court, the 5' 10" Blazejowski scored 52 points as Montclair State beat Queens College 102-91. It was the highest total by any player, male or female, since the new Garden was opened in 1968—a mark that was raised to 60 by Bernard King in 1984, but which remains the highest figure posted by a college player.

"The crowd, the excitement, it was all very stimulating," said Blazejowski, who went on to play for the 1979 World University and Pan Am Games teams. She also was a member of the 1980 U.S. Olympic squad but did not compete in Moscow due to the political boycott of the Games. She played professionally in the shortlived Women's Basketball League, where she was its leading scorer. Then she launched a career in sports marketing and worked for the National Basketball Association before being named president and general manager of the New York Liberty of the WNBA in 1997.

Nancy Lieberman-Cline: A Pioneering Woman

"For every little girl or little boy in the ghetto or on the streets, there needs to be a role model," says Nancy Lieberman-Cline, a role model for every young woman discovering the game of basketball today.

Lieberman-Cline grew up in New York and discovered basketball on the playgrounds and schoolyards of the city. "I loved the game, even though my mom didn't," she said. "She told me girls weren't supposed to play sports. I told her I was going to be the best basketball player ever. I was always told I couldn't do something because I was a girl. I had to show everyone that they were wrong."

Her basketball skill earned Lieberman-Cline a berth on the 1976 United States Olympic team. At age 18, she became the youngest player to win an Olympic medal when the United States captured the silver in the first women's Olympic basketball competition. She also earned a scholarship to Old Dominion, where she became a three-time All-American and led the Lady Monarchs to back-to-back AIAW national titles in 1979 and 1980.

A 5' 10" guard, she scored 2,430 points, grabbed 1,167 rebounds and passed for 961 assists in her college career and became the first player to twice win the Wade Trophy as Women's Player of the Year. She played in two shortlived professional leagues, the Women's Basketball League and the Women's American Basketball League, before breaking new ground in 1986 when she played for the Springfield Fame of the United States Basketball League—a summer league for men. She was the first woman to play in a men's professional league, and she did well enough to come back and play again the next season.

"I saw it as a chance to change people's perceptions about women's basketball," she explained. "I was good enough to play with the guys and start for the team; no other woman had ever done that. I think my playing in the men's league stretched the horizons for women in the future."

She later played for the Washington Generals, the team that plays against the Harlem Globetrotters, worked in sports broadcasting and marketing and made a playing comeback at age 38 with the Phoenix Mercury of the WNBA in 1997, fully 16 years after leaving Old Dominion and one year after she was elected to the Hall of Fame.

Cheryl Miller: Playing with Flair

Cheryl Miller played basketball the same way her idol, the late Pete Maravich, played the game—with style and flair.

Maravich was perhaps the game's greatest showman, a player with tremendous talent who was an entertainer as well. Like

Cheryl Miller and her teammates carry coach Pat Summitt off the court following their Olympic gold medal victory over Korea in 1984.

Maravich, Miller knew how to delight the crowd and play off its emotion, letting it carry her to greater heights.

The 6' 2" Miller, the older sister of NBA star Reggie Miller, was a four-time high school All-American who averaged 32.8 points and 15.0 rebounds for Riverside Poly High School and once scored 105 points in one game against Norte Vista High School—the top scoring performance in NCAA women's history. She was a four-time All-American at Southern Cal, leading her team to NCAA women's titles in 1983 and 1984, gaining tournament MVP honors both times, then helping the United States to the gold medal at the Olympic Games in Los Angeles that summer.

"Cheryl has revolutionized the game," declared Nancy Lieberman-Cline, a fellow Basketball Hall of Famer. "She's taught young girls to play hard all the time and to be physical. She learned to do that the same way I did—we had to play like the guys. The flamboyance is her bread and butter. She sees those cameras and she seizes the moment. Sure it's all Hollywood, but that's all right, too. I think Cheryl is the best thing that could have happened to the game."

Miller later coached at Southern Cal and is currently a commentator on TNT's coverage of the NBA. She also serves as coach and general manager of the Phoenix Mercury of the WNBA.

Ann Meyers: The Woman Who Tried Out for the NBA

Ann Meyers will forever be remembered as the first woman to try out for an NBA team, but that was only part of her legacy. She was one of the greatest players in women's basketball history, a woman whose career earned her a place in the Hall of Fame.

She was the first high school player ever chosen to the United States national team. As the first woman to receive a full athletic scholarship to UCLA, she was the first four-time All-American in women's basketball history and led the Bruins to the AIAW championship in 1978. She won a silver medal with the United States team at the 1976 Olympics, the first to include women's basketball as a medal sport. And after leaving UCLA she competed in the shortlived Women's Basketball League, twice winning MVP honors before the league folded.

Nonetheless, she received the most attention when she tried out with the Indiana Pacers in the summer of 1979. Sam Nassi, the Pacers' new owner, guaranteed her $50,000; if she didn't make the team, she could earn it by broadcasting and doing public relations work.

Though Meyers, at 5' 9" and 135 pounds, was not small by women's basketball standards, she was tiny by NBA measure, where only 5' 9" Calvin Murphy and 5' 7" Charlie Criss were her height or shorter. The signing of Meyers infuriated old-line NBAers, who thought it made a farce of the game, but they didn't have to complain for very long. In the Pacers' rookie camp it quickly became obvious that Meyers simply was too small to compete in the NBA. But when she was released at the close of camp, Pacers coach Bobby Leonard made a point of saying, "From a fundamentals standpoint, Ann is excellent. Some of the guys had better thank God that she doesn't have about six more inches and forty more pounds."

Meyers served as a broadcaster for the Pacers, competed in the Women's Basketball League and resumed her broadcasting career, working as a commentator during the first season of the WNBA. As the wife of the late baseball pitcher, Don Drysdale, she was half of sports' only Hall of Fame husband and wife team.

Lisa Leslie: 101 Points in One Half!

Among the stars of the USA Basketball Women's National Team that won the gold medal at the 1996 Olympics in Atlanta was Lisa Leslie, a 6' 5" forward/center who led the team in scoring at 19.5 points per game. But scoring points was nothing new for Leslie, who works as a professional model when she's not shooting hoops.

Despite being tall, Leslie had to be persuaded repeatedly to try the game of basketball. At first she didn't like it, but her talent soon became apparent and Leslie blossomed while in high school. Her cousin, Craig, served as her personal coach, putting her through training exercises, making her shoot baskets by herself, and pushing her to play against boys in playground games to improve her skills.

High school, college, and Olympic star **Lisa Leslie** now displays her basketball talents for the Los Angeles Sparks of the WNBA.

The work paid off. In one game for Morningside High School in Inglewood, California, she scored 101 points against South Torrance High School— and she did it in the first half alone. That has never been done by anyone else, male or female, at any level of the sport. Leslie scored 101 points in just 16 minutes. That's more than six points a minute, or one point every nine seconds!

"That was a game I'll never forget," said Leslie. "I wasn't keeping track of my points or anything, but my teammates kept passing me the ball and telling me to score. The team we were playing really wasn't very good and didn't have anybody my size, so I just kept shooting."

Leslie went on to star at Southern Cal, leading her team to the NCAA tournament in all four of her seasons and earning All-America honors three times. She played professionally in Italy before coming home to compete with the USA Basketball Women's National Team. Then she joined the Los Angeles Sparks of the WNBA.

Lobo, UConn Enjoy Dream Season

Few basketball players ever have enjoyed a season like Rebecca Lobo did in 1994–95, when she and her University of Connecticut teammates captured the hearts of a state and an entire region. Teaming with Jennifer Rizzotti, a 5' 5" junior point guard, and Kara Wolters, a 6' 7" sophomore center, the 6' 4" Lobo led Connecticut to a 35-0 record and a national championship. The Huskies joined Texas, 34-0 in 1985–86, as the only teams in NCAA history to post unbeaten seasons, and Lobo was honored as the national Player of the Year.

The Huskies' season coincided with the explosive growth in popularity of women's college basketball and helped raise it to a new level. There was a wholesome quality about Lobo and the Huskies that proved extremely appealing.

If there's one strength to point to in basketball star **Rebecca Lobo**, it's that she knows what it takes to win.

In the NCAA championship game against Tennessee, Lobo scored four consecutive baskets in the second half to help the

Huskies rally. Then Rizzotti drove the length of the court and scored with 1:51 remaining to break a 61-61 tie. The Huskies went on to win 70-64 before a paid crowd of 23,291 at the Charlotte Coliseum, the largest ever to attend an NCAA women's title game.

Lobo's dream season continued when she was named to the USA Basketball Women's National Team. Playing and practicing alongside the country's finest players, most of whom were veterans of professional ball overseas, Lobo gained valuable experience as the team won all 52 exhibition games and then swept the field en route to the Olympic gold medal at Atlanta. Lobo then joined the WNBA, competing for the New York Liberty, and stretched her personal winning streak to 102 games before finally playing on a team that lost a game.

"My life the past three years has just been incredible," said Lobo. "To be part of an undefeated team like Connecticut and win a national championship, then to compete on the national team and win an Olympic gold medal, then to have a professional league formed around me and to play in New York at Madison Square Garden, it's just incredible. It's been like a dream."

USA BASKETBALL'S WOMEN'S NATIONAL TEAM AND THE 1996 OLYMPICS

The original Dream Team, the 1992 United States Olympic team that included Michael Jordan, Magic Johnson, Larry Bird, and so many other future Hall of Famers, captured the fancy of basketball fans around the world and did more for the global growth of the sport than any other event, pushing its popularity to new levels. Four years later, another Dream Team had a similar impact on women's basketball.

In 1995, USA Basketball took the unprecedented step of bringing the country's greatest players together to form a Women's National Team that would train, practice, and compete together for a year, all leading up to the 1996 Olympics in Atlanta. With the marketing help of the National Basketball Association, major corporate sponsors were attracted to help finance this effort, paying the players and their expenses for the entire year. The result was a team that gave fans in the United States and around the world a glimpse of how well women could play the game, and won countless new fans for women's basketball.

Start with some of the best American women who had been competing in the pro leagues of Europe and Asia, players like Lisa Leslie, Katrina McClain, Ruthie Bolton, and Teresa Edwards. Add in some of the best recent college standouts, like Sheryl Swoopes and Rebecca Lobo, and you have a women's team unlike any previously assembled. They shied away from the Dream Team nickname that their male counterparts had worn since 1992, but for the members of the USA Basketball Women's National Team being a part of that squad was truly the peak of a lifelong dream.

The U.S. National Team played several exhibition games with top college programs to prepare for worldwide competition.

Women's basketball has long been played in Europe, Asia, and South America, but in the United States it has been almost nonexistent. Leagues would start up every few years, last perhaps a season or two, then fold due to lack of fan support and money. In order to make a living at the game they loved, the top college stars in the United States had to travel overseas to play professionally—or else give up playing for a career in coaching, broadcasting, or marketing.

That changed in 1995 when USA Basketball decided to bring the best players in the sport back home. After the United States women's team could do no better than a third-place finish at the 1992 Olympics and a loss to Brazil at the 1994 World

Championships, USA Basketball recognized that it needed to change the way it went about preparing for the event. With the country's top women playing on different teams in countries all over the world, USA Basketball officials saw they couldn't form an Olympic team in a matter of weeks or even months. A national team was needed, where the best players could train and play together for a significant length of time in order to ensure teamwork and cohesiveness. That's the way it's done in countless countries around the world, so why not here? The men of the NBA had enough sheer talent to overcome that lack of familiarity, but for the women a different approach was needed.

Never before had such a yearlong commitment been made, and the fact that it was made to the women's team made the initiative especially noteworthy. Tara VanDerveer, a highly successful college coach, took a one-year sabbatical from her job at Stanford to guide the team in its yearlong quest. The 11 players originally named to the team were guards Edwards, Bolton, Swoopes, Jennifer Azzi, Nikki McCray, and Dawn Staley, forwards Leslie, Lobo, McClain, and Katy Steding, and center Carla McGhee. Center Venus Lacy was later added to the team to complete the 12-player Olympic roster.

The team became a yearlong barnstorming sensation, playing games at campuses and arenas throughout the United States against the best teams in the college ranks, and making trips to Russia, the Ukraine, China, Australia, and Canada to gain international experience. They played 52 games and won all 52 of them, in the process the players raised their level of play and developed a unity and cohesiveness that no United States team had ever shown.

The United States women headed to Atlanta on a roll and proved unstoppable. Leslie scored 35 points against Japan and averaged 19.5 for the eight games, McClain averaged 8.3 rebounds, and Edwards contributed 8.0 assists per game. The United States won all eight of its games, avenging a 1994 loss to Brazil with a 111-87 victory in the gold medal game. The team also proved extremely popular, drawing crowds of over 30,000 for each of its six games at the Georgia Dome.

The success and popularity of the USA Basketball Women's National Team gave birth to not one but two professional leagues in the United States. The eight team American Basketball League played its inaugural season in the winter of 1996–97, while the eight-team WNBA (backed by the National Basketball Association) made its debut in the summer of 1997.

1996 Olympic Results

Date	Result, Leading U.S. Scorer
July 21	United States 101, Cuba 84, Lisa Leslie, 24 points
July 23	United States 98, Ukraine 65, Ruthie Bolton, 21 points
July 25	United States 107, Zaire 47, Jennifer Azzi, 18 points
July 27	United States 96, Australia 79, Katrina McClain, 24 points
July 29	United States 105, Korea 64, Nikki McCray, 16 points
July 31	United States 108, Japan 93, Lisa Leslie, 35 points
Aug. 2	United States 93, Australia 71, Lisa Leslie, 22 points
Aug. 4	United States 111, Brazil 87, Lisa Leslie, 29 points

THE AMERICAN BASKETBALL LEAGUE

The American Basketball League was the first to try to capitalize on the success of the USA Basketball Women's National Team, signing seven of its members for its inaugural 1996–97 season.

The ABL played its first season with eight franchises. From East to West, they were the New England Blizzard, Richmond Rage, Atlanta Glory, Columbus Quest, Colorado Xplosion, Seattle Reign, Portland Power, and San Jose Lasers. The ABL founders carefully chose mostly midsized markets that had shown a history of supporting women's basketball on the collegiate level, such as Richmond, Columbus, and Hartford. They also made sure that each team's roster had a distinctly local flavor—New England included Jennifer Rizzotti from Connecticut, Columbus had Ohio State's Katie Smith, Atlanta featured Georgia's Teresa Edwards, Richmond had Dawn Staley of Virginia, and San Jose featured four players from Stanford (including Olympian Jennifer Azzi) and one from Cal-Berkeley.

To increase their players' commitment, the founders gave them 10 percent of the league in return, getting them to promote the league through speaking engagements, basketball camps, and other public relations efforts. The idea was to make the ABL and its players fan-friendly, to make the players seem approachable so potential fans could identify with them.

"We feel very strongly about having the opportunity to lay the foundation and build something great for all the little girls," said Edwards, the United States' only four-time Olympic basketball player. Added Staley, another 1996 Olympian: "Little girls can dream, too. We're laying the groundwork for the six and seven-year olds. We're hoping the ABL will allow little girls who dream of playing professional basketball to attain that dream."

Throughout its inaugural season, the ABL players made sure to step back every now and then and appreciate the very fact of the league's existence. "It's great to be back home—now my mom can see me play," said Tonya Edwards of the Columbus Quest. Echoed Molly Goodenbour of the Richmond Rage, the MVP of the 1992 NCAA Final Four in her college days at Stanford: "I'm just thrilled to be a part of this. I wake up in the morning and I'm so excited to play basketball for a living. They're paying me to practice basketball, to go work out, and to play games. That's still a little hard for me to believe."

The ABL's first season was a success, if a modest one, both on and off the court. League officials conservatively set 3,000 fans per game as their attendance target, and when the 40-game season was over the league-wide average attendance was 3,536, nearly 20 percent above the target figure. Two networks gave fans at home a chance to watch ABL action, *SportsChannel* and *Black Entertainment Television.*

Fan reaction was positive and the league attracted some major sponsors including Reebok, Lady Foot Locker, Nissan, and Phoenix Home Life Insurance. New England, led by local star Rizzotti and ABL scoring champion Carolyn Jones, drew over 100,000 people to its 20 home games, a league-leading average of 5,008, and also drew the ABL's two largest crowds of the season—11,873 for a game against San Jose on January 25 and 10,477 for a game against Columbus on November 23. Hartford also was the host for the All-Star Game on December 15, when the West beat the East 81-65 before 6,387 fans.

On the court, 1996 Olympian Nikki McCray won league Most Valuable Player honors, averaging 19.9 points to lead the Columbus Quest to a 31-9 record and first place in the Eastern Conference. The Colorado Xplosion won the Western Conference with a 25-15 mark behind Defensive Player of the Year Debbie Black. In the postseason playoffs, Columbus and Richmond posted 2-0 semifinal sweeps, then Columbus won the best-of-five ABL Championship Finals 3-2 thanks to a 77-64 win in the deciding Game 5.

In preparation for the 1997–98 season, the ABL added a franchise in Long Beach, Califronia, and named Hall of Famer K. C. Jones to coach the New England Blizzard. They signed several top players including All-Americans Kate Starbird of Stanford, Kara Wolters of Connecticut, and Shalonda Enis of Alabama.

1996–97 ABL Standings

Eastern Conference

Team	W	L	Pct.
Columbus Quest	31	9	.775
Richmond Rage	21	19	.525
Atlanta Glory	18	22	.450
New England Blizzard	16	24	.400

Western Conference

Team	W	L	Pct.
Colorado Xplosion	25	15	.625
San Jose Lasers	18	22	.450
Seattle Reign	17	23	.425
Portland Power	14	26	.350

ABL POST-SEASON AWARDS

Most Valuable Player: Nikki McCray, Columbus

Coach of the Year: Brian Agler, Columbus

Defensive Player of the Year: Debbie Black, Colorado

New Pro Award: Crystal Robinson, Colorado

First Team All-ABL

Forwards: Nikki McCray, Columbus and Adrienne Goodson, Richmond

Center: Natalie Williams, Portland

Guards: Teresa Edwards, Atlanta and Dawn Staley, Richmond

Second Team All-ABL

Forwards: Cindy Brown, Seattle and Crystal Robinson, Colorado

Center: Taj McWilliams, Richmond

Guards: Debbie Black, Colorado and Carolyn Jones, New England

Playoff Results—Games

Semifinals

Columbus, two games to none over San Jose

Richmond , two games to none over Colorado

Championship

Columbus, three games to two over Richmond

MVP: Valerie Still, Columbus

THE WOMEN'S NATIONAL BASKETBALL ASSOCIATION

"We got next!"

That familiar playground phrase, signifying which group waiting to play is next in line to take on the winners of the game going on, was the marketing slogan for the launch of the Women's National Basketball Association, a summer league of eight teams backed by the NBA which held its first season in June–August 1997. *(Note: results and statistics from the WNBA's first season were unavailable at publication time.)*

Never has a women's professional basketball league had such deep pockets as this one. For several years, going back into the

This marketing slogan for the WNBA shoved male basketball players to the side and put the women at center court.

The WNBA was a great success in its innaugural season. Television ratings surpassed the projected numbers and attendance was higher than expected.

1980s, the NBA had tossed around the idea of starting up a women's league to help grow the popularity of the sport of basketball and tap into a new audience. Following the success of the USA Basketball Women's National Team and the accompanying marketing effort, league officials decided the time finally was right.

Unlike the ABL, which sought mostly midsized markets, the WNBA's eight teams were all placed in major cities. From East to West the inaugural eight were the New York Liberty, Charlotte Sting, Cleveland Rockers, Houston Comets, Utah Starzz, Phoenix Mercury, Sacramento Monarchs, and Los Angeles Sparks. Each is owned and operated by the NBA team in that city and plays its games in the NBA arena, although in some cases seating was modified to create a smaller, more intimate setting—and fewer empty seats, which the WNBA hoped would not be a problem.

"The improvement of the women's game and the success of the 1996 Olympic team took women's basketball to the next level and exposed a lot of people in a positive way to women's basketball," said Val Ackerman, the WNBA president and a former college player who served as an executive with the NBA before taking her current post. "But that hasn't been the only thing. There has been momentum building for years at the college level. The crowds have been ever-growing. And more and more girls and women are playing basketball than ever before."

And why should the WNBA succeed, when so many before it have tried and failed?

"There has never been a start-up sports league that has more resources behind it than we do," said Ackerman. "We have the full support of the NBA and all its teams. Their participation and their enthusiasm is critical to our success."

Indeed, the NBA's marketing might helped the WNBA line up major corporate sponsors such as Bud Light, Champion, General Motors, Lee Jeans, Nike, Sears Roebuck and Co., and Spalding, as well as an unprecedented women's network television package of games on NBC, ESPN, and Lifetime. A total of 32 games from the league's 115-game inaugural schedule were nationally televised, the most ever for a new league. In fact, the ability to land such an extensive television package is one reason the WNBA chose to play in the summer. "Our whole approach is based on television, which is virtually impossible to get in the fall and winter," said Hall of Famer Carol Blazejowski, a former NBA marketing executive who is president of the WNBA's New York Liberty.

Lisa Leslie and fellow Olympians Rebecca Lobo and Sheryl Swoopes were the first three players signed by the WNBA and were used extensively in marketing and television commercials to launch the new league. All were assigned by the WNBA to teams where they could capitalize on their regional appeal: Leslie with the Los Angeles Sparks, Lobo with the New York Liberty, and Swoopes with the Houston Comets.

"You'll see a level above what you're used to seeing at the college level," said Leslie prior to the WNBA's first season. "We're more aggressive, stronger, and faster. The basketball skills are on a totally different level."

Basketball fans looking for enthusiastic players who are well schooled in the game's fundamentals will find that in the WNBA, promise league officials. "There is a sheer appreciation of athleticism, of finesse, of the purity of the game," said Kelly Krauskopf, the WNBA's director of basketball operations. "If you're a fan of good athletes and execution of the game, you'll see it in the women's game. It's basketball in its simplest form, not one person overpowering another to jam it in. It's a real execution of skills. And sports fans like to watch good basketball."

Of that, there can be no argument.

HIGH SCHOOL HIGHLIGHTS

High school basketball is a part of American folklore, bridging the gap from the inner cities to the farm country to the mountain states to the plains.

It is played by about one million student-athletes annually to the delight of their fellow students, families, friends, alumni, and school supporters.

Millions flock to their local gyms to watch high school basketball, a team sport in one of its purest forms. For it is on the high school basketball courts that so many young adults, girls as well as boys, learn the values of teamwork, cooperation, and sportsmanship. They also get to experience the joy of victory and the agony of defeat, and learn how to deal with both powerful emotions.

There are approximately 17,000 member schools in the National Federation of State High School Associations from all 50 states and the District of Columbia, plus affiliate members from places like Bermuda, Canada, Guam, and the Virgin Islands. Of those schools, 16,594 had boys basketball teams and 16,198 had girls basketball teams in 1995–96, the last year for which data was available at publication time. That's a remarkable 98 percent for boys, 95 percent for girls. And according to the Federation, a total of 545,596 boys and 445,869 girls participated in competitive basketball in 1995–96. Combined it's just under one million—more than any other high school sport, including football.

In 1892, players attempted tossing the ball into a basket, much different than the one used today.

High school basketball goes back virtually to the time Dr. James Naismith had the first peach baskets nailed to the overhead running track at the YMCA Training School in Springfield, Massachusetts, on December 21, 1891. Naismith's intent was to develop an indoor game that would provide physical conditioning as well as a competitive outlet during the winter months, so it was natural that it would spread to schools in the colder regions of the country. Naismith's students took the game home with them during the winter holiday break, and soon after it was being played in high schools as far west as Chicago and Denver.

It is believed that the first interscholastic basketball game took place between Holyoke, Massachusetts, High School and Philadelphia, Pennsylvania, Central High School in 1897. Holyoke played several games that year and in 1890 won an 11-team tournament held in Boston.

The National Federation of State High School Associations was founded in 1920 with the express purpose of providing leadership for the nation's schools. To help the sport of basketball grow it has published record books, casebooks, game administration handbooks, and manuals for players and officials. In recent years it has assumed the responsibility for writing and coordinating the rules to be used in high school competition as well.

The first statewide invitational basketball tournament is believed to have been held in 1905 at Lawrence College in Appleton, Wisconsin. Tournaments like that one quickly became popular and were sponsored by colleges, civic groups, or individuals until state athletic/activity associations took them over. The first state association-sanctioned boys basketball tournaments were held in 1908 in Illinois, Kansas, and Utah. Within a dozen years, half the states in the country were running their own statewide tournaments. Today, "going to the States" is the expressed goal of students across the country as soon as they start shooting hoops.

STATE CHAMPIONSHIPS

Cheyenne Central High School in Wyoming has won more state championships (23) than any other boys high school team, with St. Anthony's of Jersey City, New Jersey, next at 20. The record for girls teams is 14 shared by three schools: Eldorado in Albuquerque, New Mexico; Pius XI in Milwaukee, Wisconsin; and Bishop Lynch in Dallas, Texas.

(Note: Those totals, as well as all other statistics in this chapter, are complete through the 1995–96 season, and were provided by the National Federation of State High School Associations, as were all records in this chapter.)

Most State Championships Won

Boys

23	Cheyenne Central, Wyoming
20	Jersey City St. Anthony's, New Jersey
19	Kansas City Wyandotte, Kansas
19	New Haven Hillhouse, Connecticut
16	Little Rock Central, Arkansas
16	Macon Lanier, Georgia
16	Phoenix Union, Arizona
16	Portsmouth, New Hampshire
16	Miami Senior, Florida
14	Mitchell, South Dakota
14	New Haven Wilbur Cross, Connecticut
14	Lincoln, Nebraska

Most State Championships Won (continued)

Girls

14	Albuquerque Eldorado, New Mexico
14	Milwaukee Pius XI, Wisconsin
14	Dallas Bishop Lynch, Texas
13	Nazareth, Texas
12	Clayton, New Mexico
11	Ada Byng, Oklahoma
11	Gulfport Harrison County, Mississippi
10	Tuba City, Arizona
9	Gloucester Catholic, New Jersey
9	Westbrook, Connecticut
9	Donalsonville Seminole, Georgia
9	Baskin, Louisiana

Most Consecutive State Titles

Boys

9	Jersey City St. Anthony's, New Jersey (1983–91)
8	Northfork, West Virginia (1974–81)
7	Sikeston Scott County Central, Missouri (1985–91)
7	Thatcher, Arizona (1980–86)
7	Snook, Texas (1978–84)
7	Providence Central, Rhode Island (1969–75)
6	Virginia City Storey County, Nevada (1962–67)
6	Houston Wheatley, Texas (1950–55)
6	Charleston, South Carolina (1921–26)
6	Albuquerque Academy, New Mexico (1989–94)

Girls

12	Milwaukee Pius XI, Wisconsin (1982–93)
8	Clayton, New Mexico (1983–90)
8	Kirtland Central, New Mexico (1980–87)
8	Monetta, South Carolina (1933–40)
8	Baskin, Louisiana (1948–55)
8	Dallas Bishop Lynch, Texas (1989–96)
7	Gulfport Harrison Central, Mississippi (1977–83)
6	Westbrook, Connecticut (1982–87)
6	Nazareth, Texas (1977–82)

THE PASSAIC WONDER TEAMS

Among the most successful boys high school basketball teams of all time were those that competed for Passaic High School in New Jersey more than 70 years ago.

On December 17, 1919, Passaic High defeated Newark Junior College 44-11 to start the 1919–20 season. That tipped off the longest winning streak in boys' scholastic basketball history—the New Jersey school would win 159 consecutive games before finally losing to Hackensack High School 39-35 on February 6, 1925.

The girls' scholastic record is held by Baskin, Louisiana High School, which won 218 games in a row from 1947 through 1953.

Passaic's teams, coached by Professor Ernest A. Blood, became known as the Passaic Wonder Teams. Blood called the 1921–22 team, that included Hall of Famer Johnny Roosma at his best. That team went 33-0 and outscored its opponents 2,293 to 612, scoring 100 points or more eight times including four games in a row. In a span of 11 days, Passaic beat Ridgewood 101-12, Eastern District 100-26, Hackensack 103-20, and Williams Prep 145-5.

"Since the center tap was used after every score, we rarely lost possession of the ball. That accounts for the lopsided scores," said Roosma. "The Professor emphasized fundamentals, and we were so thoroughly schooled and we passed so well that we seemed to hypnotize the opposition."

Roosma said he was most proud of the impact the team's streak, and the publicity it attracted, had on the growth of the young sport of basketball. "By the time we reached a hundred in a row," he said, "every newspaper in the country was publishing the results of our games. Kids began installing baskets in their backyards. They all wanted to play the game."

Passaic's 159-game streak nearly was 201 games—Passaic had won 41 straight before losing to Union Hill in the 1919 New Jersey state championship final prior to starting its record streak. "The Passaic Wonder Teams will never be forgotten and their record may never be equaled," said Hall of Fame coach Nat Holman.

Hall of Famer **Johnny Roosma** was the star of the 1921–22 Passaic High School team that coach Ernest Blood called his "best ever."

Most Consecutive Wins

Boys

159	Passaic, New Jersey (1919–25)
129	Valdosta Christian, Georgia (1979–84)
114	Wahoo, Nebraska (1988–92)
104	Belleville Central Union Academy, New York (1966–71)
103	Palmer, Iowa (1986–89)
91	Beaufort, South Carolina (1960–62)
90	Snook, Texas (1964–66)
85	Honolulu St. Louis, Hawaii (1966–68)
83	Brewster, Washington (1975–78)
83	Houston Kashmere, Texas (1974–76)

Girls

218	Baskin, Louisiana (1947–53)
154	Monetta, South Carolina (1933–40)
134	Duncanville, Texas (1987–91)
134	Butler Taylor County, Georgia (1968–72)
122	Valdosta Lowndes, Georgia (1976–81)
120	Nashua, New Hampshire (1984–89)
110	Shelbyville Central, Tennessee (1987–91)
108	Millersburg West Holmes, Ohio (1984–86)
107	Williamstown, Vermont (1947–56)
106	Midway, South Carolina (1952–56)

MILAN HIGH SCHOOL: THE REAL-LIFE HOOSIERS

In the movie *Hoosiers*, a boys basketball team from a tiny school in rural Indiana, guided by a veteran coach played by Gene Hackman, upsets the big-city school to win the state championship. Well, believe it or not, there were real-life Hoosiers, and they came from Milan High School. With an enrollment of just 161 students, Milan defeated big-city Muncie Central 32-30 to win the 1954 Indiana State Championship at Butler Fieldhouse in Indianapolis.

Muncie vs. Milan

The 1954 Indiana state final between Milan High School and Muncie Central was a true case of David vs. Goliath.

To fully appreciate this David over Goliath story, you have to know something about Hoosier Hysteria. That's the nickname given to the unbridled passion that the fanatic followers of high school basketball in Indiana display for the sport. Hoosier Hysteria reaches a peak in February and March with a huge statewide tournament, the climax of which takes place in the state capital.

Unlike most other states, where teams compete in different divisions according to school size, Indiana until recently held just one tournament that was open to all schools, big or small. Thus, the Davids of the state had a shot at the ultimate prize.

When Milan met Muncie for the title in 1954, it was at a disadvantage not only in the number of students but in the size of its players. Milan's starting center stood just 5' 11", and the tallest player on the team was 6' 2". Muncie, by contrast, had a starting front line that went 6' 5", 6' 4", and 6' 2".

The game was close and low-scoring. Two free throws by Jim Hinds put Muncie ahead 28-26 with 7:41 to play, then Milan decided to take some time off the clock and killed more than four minutes before calling a timeout. A subsequent shot by two-time All-State player Bobby Plump, a quick 5' 10" guard, was off target, but Milan pressed Muncie into a turnover and Ray Craft scored on a driving layup to tie the score.

Two free throws by Plump put the Indians ahead 30-28, but a long shot by Gene Flowers of Muncie in the final minute tied the score again. Milan coach Marvin Wood ordered his team to hold the ball for one last shot and called a timeout with 18 seconds left to map out a final play.

Wood cleared room for Plump by putting his other four players on the left side of the key. Plump was given the option of driving for the basket and shooting or, if covered, passing to one of his teammates. With five seconds left, Plump made his move. He started to drive, and as his defender backed off, not wanting to commit a foul or get beaten for a layup, Plump stopped and lofted a jumper. His shot sailed through the hoop at the buzzer, giving the real-life Hoosiers a 32-30 victory.

THE FRANKLIN WONDER FIVE

In hoop-crazy Indiana, where high school basketball is somewhere between a passion and an obsession, there has never been a more successful team than the Franklin Wonder Five, who captured the hearts of the state's fans in the 1920s.

Franklin, in south-central Indiana, first gained statewide attention in 1919 when it compiled an 18-2 record behind the play of 14-year-old freshman Robert "Fuzzy" Vandivier, a future Hall of Famer. The team lost in the state tournament, but the next year it compiled a record of 29-1 under coach Griz Wagner and won the state title.

Four of Franklin's five starters graduated that summer, so Wagner moved Vandivier to center and surrounded him with four youngsters who had played together since grade school. The five quickly developed a remarkable closeness both on and off the court. Vandivier, an outstanding passer and shooter, led them to the state title in 1921 with a 29-4 record, and the following year, before a crowd of 12,000 at the Indiana State Fairgrounds Coliseum in Indianapolis, Franklin won an unprecedented third state title in a row, capping a 31-4 season.

But the Franklin Wonder Five was not finished. Wagner became coach and athletic director at Franklin College and brought Vandivier and his four other starters along with him. They won their first game by a 69-7 count and as freshmen went 18-0 and captured the state collegiate title. They even beat one of the best professional teams in the country, the Omars—not once, but twice.

The next year they went 19-1 and repeated as state champions. As juniors, they were 17-4, though they failed to win the state title at least partly because of a rib injury suffered by Vandivier. The following year the saga of the Franklin Wonder Five came to a quiet close, as Vandivier's playing career was cut short by a painful spinal infection and Wagner was unable to coach due to eye ailments. The team went 13-6 and the dynasty was over, but it stands as the greatest run in Indiana hoops history.

Even though he could no longer play, Vandivier returned to the game of basketball following graduation and coached at Franklin High for 18 years. During 14 of those seasons, his teams won the state sectional tournament.

TEAM RECORDS—BOYS

Most Wins: Centralia, Illinois(1,780-761).

Most Overtime Periods in a Game: 13, Mamers Boone Trail, North Carolina (56) vs. Angier, North Carolina (54), February 29, 1964.

Most Points in a Season: 4,947 by Florien, Louisiana, 1979–80.

Most Points Per Game in a Season: 114.6 by Hobbs, New Mexico, 1969–70.

Most 100-Point Games in a Season: 31 by Houston Wheatley, Texas, 1972–73.

Most Consecutive 100-Point Games in a Season: 14 by Hobbs, New Mexico, 1969–70.

Most Points in a Game: 211 by De Quincy Grand Avenue, Louisiana, January 29, 1964.

Most Points by Two Teams in a Game: 290 by Sarasota Riverview, Florida (148) and Bradenton Bayshore, Florida (142), January 13, 1995.

Fewest Points in a Game: 1 by Georgetown, Illinois vs. Homer, Illinois (0), March 6, 1930, by Magnolia, Illinois vs.

Granville Hopkins, Illinois (0), November 20, 1929, and by Drain, Oregon vs. Wilbur, Oregon (0), 1927.

Highest Field Goal Percentage in a Season: .578 (1,045-for-1,807) by Chisholm, Minnesota 1981–82.

Highest Field Goal Percentage in a Game: .857 (30-for-35) by Jackson, Kentucky vs. Morgan County, Kentucky, January 19, 1982.

Most Consecutive Field Goals in a Game: 25 by Chicago Providence-St.-Mel, Illinois vs. Chicago St. Francis de Sales, Illinois, December 15, 1984.

Most Three-Point Field Goals in a Game: 24 by Kilgore Troup, Texas vs. Union Grove, Texas, February 8, 1994.

Kevin Garnett of Chicago's Farragut High School became only the fourth basketball player ever to go directly from high school to the NBA.

Most Three-Point Field Goal Attempts in a Game: 63 by Sour Lake Hardin-Jefferson, Texas vs. Hardin, Texas, February 11, 1992.

Most Three-Point Field Goals in a Season: 371 by Sour Lake Hardin-Jefferson, Texas, 1991–92.

Highest Three-Point Field Goal Percentage in a Season: .479 (58-for-121) by Ramona, California 1987–88.

Most Free Throws in a Game: 70 by Stanton Powell County, Kentucky vs. Louisville Shawnee, Kentucky, January 15, 1972.

Most Free Throw Attempts in a Game: 127 by Stanton Powell County, Kentucky vs. Louisville Shawnee, Kentucky, January 15, 1972.

Most Consecutive Free Throws: 40 by Johnstown-Monroe, Ohio (two games), 1979.

Highest Free Throw Percentage in a Season: .821 (435-for-530) by Valparaiso, Indiana, 1989–90.

Most Rebounds in a Game: 121 by Oil City Venango Christian, Pennsylvania vs. Marienville East Forest, Pennsylvania, February 20, 1970.

Most Rebounds Per Game in a Season: 57.7 by Safford, Arizona, 1972, and by Williams, Arizona, 1978.

TEAM RECORDS—GIRLS

Most Points in a Season: 3,589 by Florien, Louisiana, 1990–91.

Most Points Per Game in a Season: 93.6 by South Sioux City, Nebraska, 1995–96.

Most Points in a Game: 179 by Riverside Poly, California vs. Riverside Norte Vista, California, January 26, 1982.

Most Points by Two Teams in a Game: 217 by Conway Guy-Perkins, Arkansas (117) vs. Humphrey, Arkansas (100), October 25, 1994.

Highest Field Goal Percentage in a Season: .542 by Nashua, New Hampshire, 1987

Most Three-Point Field Goals in a Game: 17 by Grass Valley Bear River, California, February 1, 1996.

Most Three-Point Field Goal Attempts in a Game: 40 by Grass Valley Bear River, California, February 1, 1996.

Most Three-Point Field Goals in a Season: 239 by Grass Valley Bear River, California, 1995–96.

Most Free Throws Made with None Missed in a Game: 26 by Franklin Community, Indiana vs. Mooresville, Indiana, January 12, 1987.

Most Free Throw Attempts in a Game: 67 by Wilson Rivercrest, Arkansas vs. Trumann, Arkansas, February 15, 1996.

Most Free Throws in a Season: 619 by Longview, Texas 1990–91.

Highest Free Throw Percentage in a Season: .754 (347-for-460) by Waterfall Forbes Road, Pennsylvania, 1992_93.

Most Rebounds in a Game: 116 by Livonia Ladywood, Michigan vs. Riverview Gabriel Richard, Michigan, October 4, 1979.

Most Rebounds in a Season: 1,750 by Inglewood Morningside, California, 1989–90.

Most Rebounds Per Game in a Season: 68.9 by Livonia Ladywood, Michigan, 1980–81.

INDIVIDUAL RECORDS

Greg Procell of Noble Ebarb in west central Louisiana scored 6,702 career points in 1967–70, the most in scholastic history. He averaged 37.2 points per game during his career. In his senior year he scored 3,173 points and averaged 46.7 points-per-game in leading Noble Ebarb to the Louisiana Class C state title.

NBA star **Jason Kidd** still holds the high school record for most steals in a season and career while playing for Alameda St. Joseph Notre Dame High School in California.

Missy Thomas of Gibsland Gibsland-Coleman, Louisiana, holds the girls career record with 4,506 points in 1992–95. (Lynne Lorenzen of Ventura, Iowa holds the record for six-girls basketball with 6,736 career points in 1984–87.)

Boys

Most Points in a Game: 135 by Danny Heater, Burnsville, West Virginia, January 26, 1960.

Most Points in a Season: 3,173 by Greg Procell, Noble Ebarb, Louisiana, 1969–70.

Most Points Per Game in a Season: 54.0 by Bobby Joe Douglas, Marion, Louisiana, 1979–80.

Most Points in a Career: 6,702 by Greg Procell, Noble Ebarb, Louisiana, 1967–70.

Most Points Per Game in a Career: 41.1 by Steve Blehm, Devils Lake School for the Deaf, North Dakota, 1969–73.

Most Three-Point Field Goals in a Game: 21 by Chad Bickley, Santa Maria Valley Christian Academy, California, vs. Sacramento Citadel Baptist Schook California, December 28, 1994.

Most Three-Point Field Goal Attempts in a Game: 39 by Chad Bickley, Santa Maria Valley Christian Academy, California, vs. Sacramento Citadel Baptist School, California, December 28, 1994.

Most Three-Point Field Goals in a Season: 216 by Corrie Johnson, Hardin County, Texas, 1992–93.

Most Three-Point Field Goal Attempts in a Season: 514 by Cale Black, Crossville, Alabama, 1988–89.

Highest Three-Point Field Goal Percentage in a Season (minimum 100 field goals attempted): .576 (64-for-111) by Chris Vogt, Campbell Hill Trico, Illinois, 1989–90.

Most Three-Point Field Goals in a Career: 507 by Chad Bickley, Santa Maria Valley Christian Academy, California, 1992–95.

Most Three-Point Field Goal Attempts in a Career: 1,443 by Chad Bickley, Santa Maria Valley Christian Academy, California, 1992–95.

Most Free Throws in a Game: 38 by Bill Harvey, Hampton Bays, New York vs. Eastport, New York, January 19, 1979.

Most Free Throw Attempts in a Game: 45 by Bill Harvey, Hampton Bays, New York vs. Eastport, New York, January 19, 1979.

Most Consecutive Free Throws Made: 126 by Daryl Moreau, New Orleans De La Salle, Louisiana, January 17, 1978–January 9, 1979 (21 games in two seasons).

Most Free Throws in a Season: 380 by John Somogyi, New Brunswick St. Peter's, New Jersey, 1967–68.

Gene Hackman starred in the 1989 film *Hoosiers*, a popular movie about the Indiana State High School basketball tournament.

Highest Free Throw Percentage in a Season (minimum 100 free throws attempted): .975 (119-for-122) by Daryl Moreau, New Orleans De La Salle, Louisiana, 1978–79.

Highest Free Throw Percentage in a Career (minimum 300 free throws attempted): .898 (308-for-343) by Samuel Jones, St. Mary's, West Virginia, 1988–91.

Most Rebounds in a Game: 55 by Mark Barbacz, Oil City Venago Christian, Pennsylvania, February 20, 1970, and by Ryan Roberts, Downs Tri-Valley, Illinois, vs. Urbana University, Illinois, December 22, 1980.

Most Rebounds in a Season: 1,139 by Bruce Williams, Florien, Louisiana, 1979–80.

Most Rebounds Per Game in a Season (minimum 15 games): 30.8 by Lavon Mercer, Metter, Georgia, 1975–76.

Most Rebounds in a Career: 3,059 by Bruce Williams, Florien, Louisiana, 1977–80.

Most Assists in a Game: 35 by Andre Colbert, Lockport DeSales, New York, vs. Lancaster St. Mary's, New York, February 19, 1987.

Most Assists in a Season: Huey Scott, Florien, Louisiana, 1979–80.

Most Assists in a Career: Huey Scott, Florien, Louisiana, 1977–80.

Most Steals in a Game: 17 by Mark Anderson, Gonvick Gonvick-Trail, Minnesota, vs. Bagley, Minnesota, December 4, 1984.

Most Steals in a Season: 245 by Jason Kidd, Alameda St. Joseph Notre Dame, California, 1991–92.

Most Steals in a Career: 719 by Jason Kidd, Alameda St. Joseph Notre Dame, California, 1989–92.

Most Blocked Shots in a Game: 20 by Nate Holmstadt, Monticello, Minnesota vs. Waseca, Minnesota, March 18, 1995, and by Dan Hicks, Lindsay, California, vs. Orosi, California, 1975.

Most Blocked Shots in a Season: 334 by Darnell Robinson, Emeryville Emery, California, 1991–92.

Most Blocked Shots in a Career: 1,187 by Darnell Robinson, Emeryville Emery, California, 1990–93.

Girls

Most Points in a Game: 105 by Cheryl Miller, Riverside Poly, California, vs. Riverside Notre Vista, California, January 26, 1982.

Most Points in a Season: Geri Grigsby, McDowell, Kentucky, 1976–77.

Most Points Per Game in a Season: 60.0 by Christy Cooper, Circleville, West Virginia, 1988–89.

Most Points in a Career: 4,506 by Missy Thomas, Gibsland Gibsland-Coleman, Louisiana, 1992–95.

Most Points Per Game in a Career: 46.1 by Geri Grigsby, McDowell, Kentucky, 1975–77.

Most Three-Point Field Goals in a Game: 14 by Danielle Viglione, Fair Oaks Del Campo, California, vs. Rio Linda, California, January 16, 1992.

Most Three-Point Field Goals in a Season: 169 by Danielle Viglione, Fair Oaks Del Campo, California, 1991–92.

Most Three-Point Field Goal Attempts in a Season: Danielle Viglione, Fair Oaks Del Campo, California, 1991–92.

Highest Three-Point Field Goal Percentage in a Season (minimum 100 field goals attempted): .594 (60-for-101) by Christina Ortega, Phoenix Xavier, Arizona, 1987–88.

Cheryl Miller was a four-time All-American for Riverside Poly High School in California.

Most Three-Point Field Goals in a Career: 453 by Jaime Walz, Ft. Thomas Highlands, Kentucky 1993–96.

Most Three-Point Field Goal Attempts in a Career: 1,193 by Jaime Walz, Ft. Thomas Highlands, Kentucky, 1993–96.

Most Free Throws Made in a Game: 33 by Angie Sapp, Williamsville, Illinois vs. Pleasant Plains, Illinois, January 22, 1990.

Jaime Walz of Highlands High School and Daymeon Fishback of Greenwood High School pose with their trophies after being named Kentucky's Miss and Mr. Basketball in 1996.

Most Free Throws Made in a Season: 299 by Jaime Walz, Ft. Thomas Highlands, Kentucky 1994–95.

Highest Free Throw Percentage in a Season (minimum 100 free throws attempted): .885 by Jaime Walz, Ft. Thomas Highlands, Kentucky, 1995–96.

Most Rebounds in a Game: 54 by Andrea Kaehne, La Verne Calvary Baptist, California, vs. Pico Rivera Mesrobian, California, February 7, 1995.

Most Rebounds in a Season: 816 by Terri Mann, San Diego Point Loma, California, 1986–87.

Most Rebounds Per Game in a Season (minimum 15 games): 29.8 by Andrea Kaehne, La Verne Calvary Baptist, California, 1994–95.

Most Rebounds in a Career: 2,256 by Terri Mann, San Diego Point Loma, California, 1984–87.

Most Assists in a Game: 38 by Theresa Cross, Brea-Olinda, California, vs. Anaheim, California, January 13, 1987.

Most Assists in a Season: 460 by Mary Johnson, Longview, Texas, 1982–83.

Most Assists in a Career: 1,169 by Mary Johnson, Longview, Texas, 1980–83.

Most Steals in a Game: 20 by Angie Kisena, Redondo Beach Gateway Christian, California, vs. Huntington Beach Claremont, California, 1993.

Most Steals in a Season: 282 by Betsy Wilgenburg, Escondido Calvin Christian, California, 1988–89.

Most Steals in a Career: 746 by Jackie White, Fresno San Joaquin Memorial, California, 1977–80.

Most Blocked Shots in a Game: 18 by Crystal Boles, Jackson, Minnesota, vs. Madelia-Truman, Minnesota, 1992.

Most Blocked Shots in a Season: 373 by Chris Enger, Vista, California, 1987–88.

Most Blocked Shots in a Career: 1,112 by Adia Barnes, San Diego Mission Bay, California, 1991–94.

100-POINT GAMES

Danny Heater of Burnsville, West Virginia, set the scholastic scoring record by pouring in 135 points against Widen, West Virginia, on January 26, 1960. The game was played on a much smaller court than usual, measuring just 35 by 50 feet instead of the optimum 50 by 84 feet or 50 by 94 feet. Burnsville played a pressure defense and Heater's teammates constantly fed him the ball in an effort to help him impress scouts and earn a college scholarship.

Former Inglewood Morningside High School standout **Lisa Leslie** not only stars in the WNBA, she is a professional fashion model.

100 Point Game Players

Boys

Points	Player, School, Date
135	Danny Heater, Burnsville, West Virginia, 1/26/60
127	Johnny Morris, Portsmouth Norcom, Virginia, 2/22/61
120	Dick Bogenrife, Sedalia Medway, Ohio, 2/6/53
114	Pete Cimino, Bristol, Pennsylvania, 1/22/60
114	Wayne Oakley, Hanson, Kentucky, 12/2154
108	Ken Robinson, Cassatt Midway, South Carolina, 1961
108	Morris Dale Mathis, St. Joe, Arkansas, 1/25/55
105	Kenneth Johnson, Grandfield, Oklahoma, 1/1079
104	Danny Boyd, Camden, Tennessee, 1/6/61
103	Dickie Pitts, Wimauma, Florida, 2/14/56
102	Bennie Fuller, Little Rock School for the Deaf, Arkansas, 12/4/71
100	Greg Procell, Noble Ebarb, Louisiana, 1/29/70

Girls

Points	Player, School, Date
105	Cheryl Miller, Riverside Poly, California, 1/25/82
101	Lisa Leslie, Inglewood Morningside, California, 2/7/90

Heater scored 53 points in the first half and 82 in the second half. He shot 53-for-70 from the field and 29-for-41 from the free throw line—and yes, he did earn that scholarship, to the University of Richmond.

One of the most amazing scoring feats in scholastic basketball history was turned in by Lisa Leslie of Inglewood Morningside, California, in a game against South Torrance High School of Torrance, California, on February 7, 1990.

The 6' 5" Leslie, who would later star for Southern California and for the United States' gold medal team at the 1996

Olympics in Atlanta, scored 101 points in the game. What's more, she got all 101 points in the first half—the South Torrance team refused to play the second half. Besides being the second-highest scoring girls' player on record, behind Cheryl Miller's 105 points, Leslie's 101-point half is a record and her two quarters of 52 and 49 points are tops as well.

Heater and Leslie are two of 12 boys and two girls who have recorded 100-point games in interscholastic competition (it also was done 19 times in six-girl basketball). Here is the list.

Cheryl Miller: Riverside's Record-Setter

Before she became a three-time national Player of the Year at the University of Southern California and a member of the United States team that won a gold medal at the 1984 Olympics in Los Angeles, Cheryl Miller was a scoring sensation for Riverside Poly, California.

Miller led Riverside Poly to 84 consecutive wins, four California Interscholastic Federation—Southern Section championships, the 1981–82 state title and a 31-0 record in her senior year. She established a girls single-game scoring record by pouring in 105 points against Riverside Norte Vista, California, on January 26, 1982. Miller averaged over 30 points per game for three straight seasons, but she was more than just a scorer—her 672 rebounds in 1981–82 are the second-highest single-season total on record.

In 1997 Miller coached the Phoenix Mercury in the inaugural season of the Women's NBA, while also serving as an analyst on TNT telecasts of NBA games.

All In the Family

John Somogyi of New Brunswick St. Peter's scored 3,310 points from 1965–68 to become the leading scorer in New Jersey high school basketball history. His record was broken by his own daughter, Kristen Somogyi, who scored 3,899 points for New Brunswick St. Peter's from 1989–92.

The number 24 figured prominently for both father and daughter. Both wore jersey Number 24, and John's record stood for 24 years before it was broken by his daughter.

Michael Jordan's Slow Start

Michael Jordan always was proud that his younger brother Larry Jordan was the star player on the Laney High School basketball team. Michael worked hard on his game to try to be like his brother, but could never beat him one-on-one. However, when his father, James Jordan, saw the drive and determination in Michael, he built a court in their backyard so the boys could practice at home. Young Michael quickly wore away the grass.

"We played neighborhood games for at least two hours every day, and on Saturdays we were out there all day," said Jordan, who credits playing with older boys as helping to improve his game.

"Larry always used to beat me on the backyard court," Jordan said. "His vertical jump is higher than mine. He's got the dunks and some three-sixties and most of the same stuff I have. And he's only five-seven. He's my inspiration."

When Michael Jordan tried out for the Laney varsity team, he was less than six feet tall and his skills had not yet been developed. He didn't make the team—Michael Jordan, possibly the greatest basketball player who ever lived, was cut from his high school team as a sophomore by Coach Fred Lynch.

Michael Jordan didn't make the varsity squad until his junior year in high school. It was from that point on that "His Airness" took flight.

Jordan did not give up. He averaged 27 points per game for the junior varsity team and hoped for a call-up to the varsity, but it never came. When the team qualified for the state regionals, the only reason Jordan got to go was because one of the student managers got sick.

"I had to carry the uniform of the star player to get in," Jordan recalled. "I never wanted that to happen again. From that day on, I just worked at my basketball skills."

Jordan became obsessed with making the team, to the point where he neglected his schoolwork. His father set him straight, telling him he'd never achieve his goal of a college scholarship if he didn't improve his studies. "I knew he was right and I tried to change," said Jordan. "I concentrated more on my schoolwork."

Jordan found the right balance between his schoolwork and athletics, and over the summer something special happened: he grew four inches and stood 6' 3" by the time his junior year began. Jordan not only made the team, but earned a place in the starting lineup. His hard work had paid off, and his career was on its way.

SIX-GIRL BASKETBALL

When Senda Berenson Abbott adapted James Naismith's original basketball rules for women in 1892, she did it with the idea of discouraging roughness. So she divided the court into three equal sections, and players were not permitted to leave their section. Another set of rules, developed in 1895 by Clara Gregory Baer in New Orleans, divided the court according to the number of players on a team and restricted each player to her own section.

At a meeting in Springfield in 1899, a Women's Basketball Committee was formed to develop a unified set of rules, and they adopted Abbott's rules—no surprise, since she was a member of the committee. However, Baer's rules remained popular in the south, where they were used as late as 1922. The number of players on a side varied between five and ten, although six was most common.

In the 1930s some teams began experimenting with a two-court game—dividing the court into two sections instead of three, giving each player a little more room. This proved extremely popular. In 1938 the two-court game became the official girls game, with six players on a team, three guards and three forwards. Only the forwards could score.

So while boys were playing five to a side, girls were playing six to a side with the court divided in half and players restricted to their sections. That's the way it remained until the 1960s, when two of the six players were designated as "rovers" and permitted to move between sections and play over the full court in order to "provide more opportunity for team play and encourage all players to develop skills of shooting and both defensive and offensive tactics."

In 1969, experimental use of five-player teams playing a full-court game was permitted for the first time, in conjunction with a 30-second shot clock. This proved extremely popular and was continued for a second year, and in 1971 it was made official—bringing girls basketball in line with the boys game. But some states, notably Iowa and Oklahoma, continued to play six-girl basketball for another two decades. In Iowa, for example, schools did not begin to phase in five-girl basketball until 1984, and the six-girl game was not totally phased out until 1994.

Because only three players were permitted to shoot, the scores of six-girl basketball tended to be higher than those for the five-girl game. Also, individual scoring averages and shooting percentages tended to be higher, since only the best shooters played at the offensive end of the court. As a result, some amazing records were set in six-girl basketball, records that surpass those for the five-girl game.

For example, Geri Grigsby's single-season record of 1,885 points in five-girl basketball was surpassed three times in six-girl play, twice by Denise Long and once by Lynne Lorenzen. And the 100-point single-game plateau has been reached 19 times in six-girl basketball and only twice in five-girl play.

Coaching Records

Boys

Wins	Coach, School, Years
1,096	Bill Krueger, Cameron Cameron-Yoe, Texas, San Marcos, Texas, League City Clear Creek, Texas, Houston Clear Lake, Texas, 1958–96
1,093	Morgan Wootten, Hyattsville DeMatha, Maryland, 1957–96
1,090	Robert Hughes, Ft. Worth, I.M. Terrell, Texas, Ft. Worth Dunbar, Texas, 1958–96
1,081	Ralph Tasker, Sulpher Springs, Ohio, Lovington, New Mexico, Hobbs, New Mexico, 1941–96
1,026	Leslie Gaudet, Pine Prairie, Louisiana, 1947–70

Girls

Wins	Coach, School, Years
1,217	Jim Smiddy, Charleston, Tennessee, Cleveland Bradley Central, Tennessee, 1948–93
1,152	Bertha Teague, Ada Byng, Oklahoma, 1928–70
1,063	Thednall Hill, Hardy Highland, Arkansas, 1952–86
953	Leta Andrews, Granbury, Texas, 1962–96
943	Dean Weese, Higgins, Texas, Spearman, Texas, Levelland, Texas, 1958–96

THE DREAM TEAM AND THE GLOBAL GAME

Basketball has been popular around the world almost since its beginning, as Naismith's students took word of his game far and wide.

It is estimated than more than 300 million people—young and old, girls and boys—are playing the sport regularly, and there are professional leagues throughout Europe, South America, Asia, and Australia as well as North America. Basketball reached around the world at the 1936 Olympics, when it first became a medal sport, and took a quantum leap with the popularity of the star-studded Dream Team that won the gold medal for the United States at the 1992 Olympics in Barcelona.

A POPULAR BUNCH

The Dream Team, including such greats as Michael Jordan, Magic Johnson, Larry Bird, and Charles Barkley, truly was an international sensation. The players were mobbed by fans wherever they went. Hundreds waited outside the team's hotel in Barcelona at all hours of the day and night, hoping to catch a glimpse of their heroes. When Barkley went for a midnight stroll down Las Ramblas, the city's main tourist street, he was like the Pied Piper, drawing fans of all ages in his wake. When

As good as the 1992 Olympic basketball team was, **Charles Barkley** still managed to get a technical foul here against Croatia.

Jordan went to the boxing site to watch the competition, the match in progress had to be halted because of all the commotion that surrounded his entrance. When Jordan went to play golf, he attracted the kind of galleries you see on the PGA tour. And when many of the basketball players chose to participate in the Olympics' Opening Ceremony, athletes from other countries broke ranks to try to get an autograph, a handshake, a photograph, or just to see the members of the Dream Team up close.

Basketball actually was first played at the Olympics in 1904, barely more than a decade after the sport was invented. Five teams, all from the United States, competed at the Summer Olympics in St. Louis, where basketball was a demonstration sport—a non-medal event added to the Olympic program at the request of the host nation. Basketball then disappeared from the Olympics until 1936 in Berlin, Germany, when it made its debut as a competitive, medal sport.

Twenty-two nations entered that first competition, though only 21 competed—Spain had to withdraw due to the civil war in that country. The United States team, made up primarily of players from two corporate-sponsored teams representing Universal Pictures of Hollywood, California, and Globe Oil and Refining of McPherson, Kansas, was heavily favored to win the gold medal and did not disappoint. The Americans overpowered the competition, winning every game easily. In the gold medal game, they beat Canada 19-8 playing on an outdoor clay court that turned into mud due to heavy rains.

The fact that the first Olympic basketball competition drew more entries than any other sport at the 1936 Olympics showed the sport's growing global popularity. As *The New York Times* noted, "It is now clear that basketball no longer is merely an American game, but a genuine world game."

The 1936 U.S. Olympic basketball team captured the gold medal in the sport's first year as an Olympic event.

Basketball became a popular attraction at the large sporting clubs that are so much a part of European life. These clubs often have thousands of members, and they form teams to compete against teams from similar clubs in other cities. These sporting clubs often develop intense rivalries, such as that between Real Madrid and F. C. Barcelona of Spain. Their teams are the equivalent of the professional teams that compete in the United States in leagues such as the NBA.

THE NBA OVERSEAS

In order to gain an upper hand in these rivalries, these clubs allied themselves with major corporate sponsors, thus obtaining the financial support to bid for the best available players—not only in their own cities or regions, but throughout their countries and in other countries as well. By the 1960s they were signing American players, not quite of NBA caliber, but players who had competed collegiately and wanted to continue their careers, often hopeful of earning a chance at the NBA. These "imports" were generally limited to two per team. This would allow the majority of roster spots to go to native-born players whose skills hopefully would improve by playing alongside the more talented players brought in from the United States.

Michael Jordan, Patrick Ewing, and **Scottie Pippen** celebrate the Dream Team's Olympic dominance.

By the 1980s, these rivalries had grown to the point where players could earn the local equivalent of hundreds of thousands of dollars per year by playing in Europe. For aging NBA players, fringe players, or young players uncertain of their future in the NBA, the leagues in Spain, Italy, Greece, and France, among other nations, presented an attractive alternative. Leagues elsewhere around the world, including South America, Australia, and Asia, began to grow and attract American players as well, though not of the talent level as those who went to Europe.

Overseeing the global growth of basketball was the International Basketball Federation. It had been formed in 1932 by the national federations of eight European countries, but it now includes some 200 members. The mandate of FIBA (the "A" stood for amateur, but when restrictions against federations that in-clude professionals as members were dropped in 1989, the original acronym was kept) was to oversee and promote the sport of basketball worldwide. It controls and governs all international competitions, including the World Championships and the Olympic basketball competition, establishes the rules and specifications for equipment and facilities, controls and governs the appointment of international referees, and regulates the transfer of players from one country to another.

NO MEDALS FOR NBA PLAYERS

It was FIBA that determined which basketball players would be eligible for events such as the Olympics, and for years it permitted players from top European club teams to compete even though they were professionals in every sense of the word, while barring NBA players from participating. FIBA also permitted players from government-supported clubs in socialist countries to compete—only NBA players were barred. The thinking was that NBA players were so skilled, they would make a shambles of the Olympics should they be permitted to compete.

Even without NBA players, the United States dominated the Olympics, winning every gold medal and every game it played from 1936 through 1968. It wasn't until the controversial gold medal game against the Soviet Union in 1972 that the United States suffered its first loss (see chapter 8). That loss, because of its disputed nature, was considered a fluke, but when the United States lost at the 1988 Olympics in Seoul, Korea, it became clear that the quality of play in the rest of the world was catching up.

One reason was the existence of year-round national teams in just about every country but the United States. The top players in various countries, in addition to competing for their clubs against each other, were also members of their countries' national teams. They would train and practice together when they were not with their individual clubs, and compete together in international events such as the Olympics. As a result they developed a teamwork and rapport that the United States team, a hastily assembled group of college players and other amateurs, did not have. This was a major factor in over-coming the advantage the United States teams had in terms of pure talent.

During the 1970s and 1980s, however, distinctions between amateurs and professionals in many sports became blurred and eventually were elimi-nated. This movement, plus the United States' loss to the Soviet Union in the 1988 Olympics, spurred FIBA to change its rules in 1989 and permit the NBA to join USA Basketball, the national gov-erning body that was the United States' representative to FIBA. As a result, NBA players would now be eligible to com-pete in FIBA events, beginning with the 1992 Olympics.

Members of the Dream Team celebrate their 116-48 drubbing of Angola during the 1992 Olympics in Barcelona.

THE BEST EVER

The team that was assembled for the Barcelona Olympics was indeed a Dream Team. Start with three of the greatest players who ever lived: Jordan, Johnson, and Bird. Add eight more NBA All-Stars: Barkley, Clyde Drexler, Patrick Ewing, Karl Malone, Chris Mullin, Scottie Pippen, David Robinson, and John Stockton. Complete the group with the top college player of 1991–92 and a future NBA All-Star, Christian Laettner.

It's no wonder it was considered the greatest team ever assembled, not only in basketball but in any team sport.

Chuck Daly was selected to be the head coach of the 1992 Olympic team. At times, he was simply a spectator watching the best players in the world.

And the reception it got was remarkable. It is hard for fans in the United States to understand the sensation the Dream Team created in Barcelona and throughout Europe among fans whose only previous exposure to these NBA superstars was through occasional telecasts of league games or highlights. "It was," said Dream Team coach Chuck Daly, "like Elvis and the Beatles put together. Traveling with the Dream Team was like traveling with twelve rock stars, that's all I can compare it to."

Indeed, they were the kings of basketball and they dominated their opposition, winning their eight games on the way to the gold medal by an average of nearly 44 points. "Dream Team is a lot of name to live up to," said Daly, "but if anything, the 1992 U.S. Olympic men's basketball team exceeded all hopes and expectations. I think we truly gave the world a glimpse—only a glimpse, since we were never seriously challenged—of what basketball can be like at its highest level."

The lopsided nature of the competition didn't surprise anybody or discourage anybody. Opposing players were happy just to be on the court with these basketball icons, true heroes of the sport. In one game, a player who was guarding Johnson suddenly started waving frantically to his team's bench—not for help from his coach, but to make sure a teammate with a camera got a picture of him and the legendary Magic.

"They knew they were playing the best in the world," said Daly. "They'll go home and for the rest of their lives be able to tell their kids, 'I played against Michael Jordan and Magic Johnson and Larry Bird.' And the more they play against our best players, the more confident they're going to get."

Subsequent editions of the Dream Team went on to win gold medals at the 1994 World Championship of Basketball in Toronto, Canada, and the 1996 Olympics in Atlanta, Georgia. But in each event the level of play by opposing teams got better and better, and it's only a matter of time before some national team does what the Soviet Union did in 1972 and upsets the mighty United States.

The original Dream Team was a landmark in basketball's global growth, winning millions of fans for the sport with its brilliance and charisma on and off the court. Basketball had been growing in global popularity for many years, but the attention that team received on the Olympic stage gained credence for basketball's claim to be closing in on soccer as the most popular sport in the world. Indeed, according to at least one survey, by 1996 more people were playing basketball than any other sport in the world.

The Global Game

Basketball has become a sport that is played and enjoyed around the world. The NBA, and more specifically the Dream Team, have played a significant role in the spread of its popularity.

NICKNAMES 7

One of the many great things about sports is its treasury of nicknames. Only in sports are the people at the very top of their profession known by the kinds of names kids tag each other with on playgrounds.

Let's face it. Your math teacher is not likely to be called Magic, Dr. J, the Dream, or the Mailman.

Sports stars become household names around the world. Very often they are known simply by one name—or by their nickname. Mention "Michael" anywhere in the world, and if the topic is sports, chances are no last name will be necessary. And it's even more so with nicknames.

It's always been that way and it always will be, because that's the way we want it to be. Sports help young fans live out their fantasies and older fans recapture their youth. Referring to superstars by their nicknames or by a single recognizable name helps us feel closer to them, even if we've only seen them in an arena or on TV.

Nicknames can come from any number of sources. Some might refer to a physical trait or characteristic such as height, as in basketball pioneer Charles "Stretch" Murphy or Elvin "The Big E" Hayes. Or the nickname might come from hair color, as in Hall of Fame coaches Arnold "Red" Auerbach and William "Red" Holzman (whose hair had turned gray by the time he finished his career). Others can be plays on their real names, such as Walt Bellamy's "Bells" or Alonzo Mourning's "'Zo." Some players get their nicknames during childhood, while others pick them up in high school, college, or the pros. Some nicknames come from relatives or friends, others from teammates, rival players, or members of the media.

It's always interesting to try to guess the source of a nickname. Some are obvious, but others are a little harder to figure out. You might guess that 6' 1" Nate Archibald, who in 1973 became the only man ever to lead the NBA in scoring and assists in the same season, was nicknamed "Tiny" because of his stature. Actually it's a bit more complicated: His dad was nicknamed "Big Tiny" and he was dubbed "Little Tiny," but once he became famous it was shortened.

Some nicknames and their origins are not obvious at all. Who decided Anfernee Hardaway was worth a "Penny" and not a "Nickel"? Why is Tyrone Bogues called "Muggsy"? How did Anthony Webb come to be known as "Spud"? Who put the "Magic" in Earvin Johnson, or gave the doctorate to Julius "Dr. J" Erving?

Nicknames often come from friends or teammates, and only they can explain them. For example, during his years with the New York Knicks, Gerald Wilkins was known as "Doug." How do you get from Gerald to Doug? Because Wilkins liked (and did a good imitation of) rap musician Doug E. Fresh. Unless you were a member of the Knicks or asked someone close to the team, that would be a hard one to guess.

The NBA has a long history of colorful nicknames. Two great early playmakers, Bob Cousy and Dick McGuire, were known as "the Houdini of the Hardwood" and "Tricky Dick," respectively, because of their ballhandling wizardry. Harry "The Horse" Gallatin was a tough customer under the boards, while "Easy" Ed Macauley made the game look effortless with his smooth skills. And would anyone want to tangle with either "Jungle" Jim Loscutoff or Larry "Mr. Mean" Smith under the boards?

Nicknames are cool, no doubt about it. But none was as cool as that belonging to four-time scoring champion George Gervin, who starred for the San Antonio Spurs in the 1970s and 1980s. Gervin was known as "The Iceman," or just plain "Ice," because he always looked so calm and unflappable on the court, showing absolutely no emotion as he buried one 20-footer after another.

For fans of Snow White, the NBA has included on its rosters Eric "Sleepy" Floyd, Harold "Happy" Hairston, and Glenn "Doc" Rivers. For bean fans, the league also has known Bob "Butterbean" Love and Joe "Jellybean" Bryant. Other nicknames include "Jumpin' Joe" Fulks, "Pogo Joe" Caldwell, "Pistol Pete" Maravich, and Chuck "The Rifleman" Connors, though the latter wasn't known by that nickname until he starred in a TV Western of the same name in the 1950s. Chuck Person is nicknamed "The Rifleman," too, and not just because he likes to shoot it up as soon as he leaves the locker room. His mom was a big fan of Connors' TV show, and as a result her son's full given name is Chuck Connors Person.

Good nicknames often get recycled, as in Dean "The Dream" Meminger and Hakeem "The Dream" Olajuwon, or the NBA's two "Kangaroo Kids," Jim Pollard from the 1940s and 1950s and Billy Cunningham from the 1960s and 1970s, both of whom are in the Hall of Fame.

There are other nicknames you wouldn't want to recycle, like Jim "Bad News" Barnes or Billy "The Whopper" Paultz (so named because of his pudgy physique). And it took Charles Barkley many years to live down "The Round Mound of Rebound."

Muggsy Bogues scurries away from Boston Celtic Artis Gilmore after stripping him of the basketball. Gilmore got a first-hand lesson on why Tyrone Bogues was nicknamed "Muggsy."

Oscar Robertson was simply known as "The Big O."

Sometimes initials make good nicknames. Adrian Dantley became known as A.D. and Kevin Johnson as K.J.

Many great players picked up nicknames in college that followed them through their pro careers. Marvin Webster was such a good shotblocker at Morgan State that he was dubbed "The Human Eraser," and the nickname stayed with him even though he never enjoyed quite the same success during his pro career with Seattle and New York.

Playgrounds often are the breeding grounds of nicknames. Unfortunately, some of the greatest stars of playground ball fall to the temptations of street life and never get to show their skills to wider audiences. One such player was Herman Knowings, a New York playground star of the 1960s who was nicknamed "Helicopter" because when he jumped he seemed to hover in midair, like a helicopter.

Style of play often leads to nicknames. Chet Walker could really run the floor, so he became "Chet the Jet." Dick Barnett used to step back in his follow-through after taking a jump shot, so he was called "Fall Back Baby." You couldn't stop Len "Truck" Robinson once he got it in gear going for a rebound, and you couldn't keep up with David "The Skywalker" Thompson once he became airborne en route to the hoop.

You don't have to be a great player to have a great nickname. Otherwise, we'd never have heard of Robert "Bubbles" Hawkins, Maurice "Toothpick" McHartley, or John "Crash" Mengelt, so nicknamed because of his nightly leaps into the courtside seats and press tables while chasing down loose balls. As for "Toothpick," who played in the ABA, he had this rather unsafe habit of keeping a toothpick in his mouth while he played—kids, do not try this at home.

Want some more great nicknames? Try matching these players with their nicknames (answers at end of chapter):

Cedric Maxwell	The Big O
Artis Gilmore	The Animal
Gus Johnson	Poodles
Bobby Smith	Butterbean
Earl Monroe	Hound
Greg Anderson	Dr. Dunk
Wayne Rollins	Dr. Dunkenstein
Glenn Robinson	Worm
Jamaal Wilkes	Hondo
Dennis Rodman	Sweetwater
Nat Clifton	Tree
Jerry Baskerville	Silk
Darrell Griffith	A Train
Ken Bannister	Honeycomb
Bill Willoughby	The Pearl
Oscar Robertson	Bingo
Bob Love	Big Dog
John Havlicek	Cadillac
Darnell Hillman	Cornbread

Team names can have interesting nicknames, too. Many got their names as a result of fan contests, and often the name bears an association to where the team plays. The Phoenix Suns are located in Arizona's Valley of the Sun, the Philadelphia 76ers play in the city where the Declaration of Independence was signed in 1776, the Denver Nuggets play in a region where gold and silver mining was once prominent, and the Miami Heat, well, let one of the franchise's founders, Zev Bufman, explain: "Heat represented the area. We're Miami. When you think of Miami, that's what you think of."

Some carry a historical context. The Detroit Pistons were originally the Fort Wayne Zollner Pistons, so named because their owner, Fred Zollner, ran a company in Fort Wayne, Indiana that made pistons for engines. The Atlanta Hawks began as the Tri-Cities Blackhawks. The three cities were Moline and Rock Island, Illinois and Davenport, Iowa and they were named for Chief Black Hawk, whose tribe was located in Rock Island. The nickname was shortened to Hawks when the team moved to Milwaukee and remained the same when the team moved to St. Louis and finally Atlanta.

Boston founder Walter Brown chose Celtics as his team's name because of the large Irish population in Boston, and because the name had a basketball tradition from a well-known barnstorming team from the 1920s called the Original Celtics. There's no definitive record of why the New York team became the Knickerbockers (and Knicks for short), but most people believe it came from the old Dutch settlement in New York and a fictional character known as Mr. Knickerbocker, as well as the style of pants worn in that era.

Franchises occasionally move, and some names travel better than others. San Diego chose Rockets because it reflected the theme of a growing city in motion with space-age industry. The name works equally well in Houston because that city is the home to NASA and the country's space program. But have you ever seen a lake in Los Angeles, or heard jazz in Utah?

Both those names are carryovers from previous homes. The Lakers began their existence in Minneapolis, the largest city in Minnesota, the state whose motto is "The Land of 10,000 Lakes." The team simply kept the name when it moved to Los Angeles in 1960. And while it was natural for New Orleans to call its expansion team the Jazz, since that music is so much a part of the Louisiana city's fabric, it seems incongruous in Mormon-oriented Salt Lake City, the team's home since 1979.

Sometimes names are changed for reasons of social concern. When people became sensitized to the feelings of Native Americans, many colleges changed names that were considered by some to be offensive—the Stanford Indians became the Cardinals and the St. John's Redmen became the Red Storm.

For many years the NBA franchise representing the nation's capital was named the Bullets. At first they were the Baltimore Bullets, then for one year they were known as the Capital Bullets before becoming, in 1974, the Washington Bullets. However, owner Abe Pollin became uncomfortable with the team's name, because even though it was meant to reflect speed, it also carries a violent implication as a form of ammunition. Pollin thought this inappropriate in light of increasing gang violence and weapons-related crimes, and the team launched a contest for a new name. The winner was Wizards, so beginning in the 1997–98 season when the team moves to its new downtown arena, it will be known as the Washington Wizards.

Here are some more basketball nicknames, and the stories behind them:

The Big Dipper: Wilt Chamberlain, perhaps the most dominating offensive player in basketball history, liked this nickname much better than "Wilt the Stilt," which a sports writer gave him during his pro career. When Chamberlain, who grew to be 7' 1", was 10 years old, he bumped his head while going through a doorway. He was told he had to dip to get through, and friends soon started calling him "Dip" or "Dippy," which soon became "The Dipper." He finally topped out as "The Big Dipper," which also is a reference to the constellation of stars in the sky. Legendary Philadelphia public address announcer Dave Zinkoff termed Chamberlain's stuff shots "Dipper Dunks."

Band-Aid: Derrick Chievous, who played college ball at Missouri and later played in the NBA, always wore a Band-Aid for good luck, hence his nickname.

Bevo: Clarence Francis scored 116 points during one game of his college career, 113 points in another, and is known to all as "Bevo." The nickname came from his father and originally was "Beeve" after a soft drink, then eventually became "Bevo."

The Round Mound of Rebound: Charles Barkley got this nickname while he was at Auburn University. Even though he stood less than 6' 5", Barkley's weight was anywhere from 250 pounds on up toward 300. Nevertheless, he was one of the most effective rebounders in college ball, so he was tabbed "The Round Mound of Rebound." It's not much of a surprise that he never liked the nickname, preferring the "Sir Charles" nickname he picked up during his professional career. That one came after he made a television commercial for a deodorant in which he portrayed an upper class gentleman at a hunt.

Muggsy: Tyrone Bogues stands only 5' 3", yet he was a star in high school and college and has enjoyed a very successful pro career, proving there's a place in basketball for players of any size if they have the talent and the heart. Perhaps because he's so easy for kids to relate to, Bogues is the most popular player on the Charlotte Hornets and one of the best-liked around the NBA. When growing up in Baltimore, Bogues was so quick and adept at stealing the ball that a friend said it was like he was mugging you. From that evolved "Muggsy."

Slick: Donald Watts was a quick guard for the Seattle Super-Sonics in the 1970s who led the NBA in steals in 1975–76. Watts

Charles Barkley has slimmed down since his younger days when he was labeled "The Round Mound of Rebound." Barkley may have lost some weight, but he certainly hasn't lost his ability to rebound.

was a fan favorite not only because of his play but because of his shaved head—he went the no-hair route long before it became popular—and thus he was nicknamed "Slick."

Big Country: Bryant Reeves's nickname makes a lot of sense. His teammate at Oklahoma State, Byron Houston, took one look at Reeves, who comes from the tiny town of Gans, Oklahoma, and said, "You're big and you're from the country. You're Big Country." The nickname stuck and soon kids all over the state were imitating Reeves's flat-top hair style.

Penny: Anfernee Hardaway was nicknamed "Penny" by childhood friends because his grandmother used to call him "Pretty," and with her southern drawl it sounded like "Penny." He makes a pretty penny these days as the star guard of the Orlando Magic.

The Human Highlight Film: Dominique Wilkins quickly became known for his spectacular dunks while at the University of Georgia, plays that made perfect video clips for the nightly sports reports— remember, this was before *SportsCenter*! Soon he was "The Human Highlight Film," since it seemed like his every play was made for the highlight reel. Wilkins also goes by the nicknames "'Nique" and "'Zoid," the latter coming from the teen term *freakazoid*.

Dominique Wilkins is one of the most acrobatic players in the NBA. He's best known for his high-flying slam dunks over defenseless opponents.

The Black Hole: Kevin McHale is now the general manager of the Minnesota Timberwolves, but before that he was a high-scoring forward for the Boston Celtics. His teammates often kidded him about the number of shots he took and nicknamed him the Black Hole, because once they threw the ball in to him, it never came back out.

Zeke from Cabin Creek: Jerry West needed a nickname. At least Elgin Baylor, his teammate on the Los Angeles Lakers, thought so. West came from Cheylan, West Virginia, but the town was so small the nearest post office was in Cabin Creek. Since Baylor called all hillbillies Zeke, West became "Zeke from Cabin Creek." One of the greatest shooters and all-around guards in NBA history, West much preferred the nickname "Mr. Clutch," a tribute to his ability to produce in pressure-packed situations.

The Admiral: David Robinson never achieved such a lofty ranking during his two-year service in the United States Navy, but for a player of his skill, "The Admiral" is much more appropriate than "The Ensign" or "The Lieutenant."

Blue: Theodore Edwards got his nickname because when he was a baby, an older sister found him choking, and his face was starting to turn blue. Edwards recovered, but the incident gave him a nickname that lasted all the way to the NBA.

Tricky Dick: Dick McGuire was one of the best passers, dribblers, and ballhandlers in the early years of the NBA. He often

Robinson Leads His Troops

After serving two years for the U.S. Navy, David Robinson was nicknamed, "The Admiral." His ability on the court has earned the respect of teammates and opponents on command.

passed up open shots, preferring to pass the ball to teammates so they could score. Since he could never be counted on to do the expected, McGuire was dubbed "Tricky Dick." It should be noted that he got the nickname more than a decade before it was applied to politician Richard M. Nixon, who eventually became president in 1968.

"Dollar" **Bill Bradley** signed one of the biggest contracts of his time, earning $400,000 as a rookie for the New York Knicks.

Dollar Bill: Bill Bradley got this nickname long before he worried about economic issues as a United States senator or in his present status as politician at large. Bradley became known as "Dollar Bill" in his days as a New York Knick after signing a multiyear contract for the then-royal sum of $400,000 as a rookie. Some of his teammates joked that it was really because he was so cheap he still had the first dollar he ever made. While he was at Princeton, Bradley was sometimes called "Mr. President" or "The Secretary of State" by teammates.

The Houdini of the Hardwood: Bob Cousy was nicknamed after Harry Houdini, a famous magician in the early part of the twentieth century who was known for his sleight of hand. Because he was such a magician at handling the basketball, Cousy got the nickname while at Holy Cross, and it stayed with him through his great career with the Boston Celtics.

Satch: Tom Sanders played a key role in the Boston Celtics dynasty that accounted for eight straight NBA titles and 11 in 13 years. He was an outstanding defender who always guarded the opposing team's high scorer, and he also was a good clutch shooter. Sanders, an avid baseball fan, got the nickname "Satch" while growing up because of a facial and physical resemblance to famed pitcher Satchell Paige.

Dr. J: Julius Erving got his nickname "Dr. J" long before he hit the national spotlight, yet it served him well once he reached the big time. While growing up in Roosevelt, New York, Erving

had a friend with whom he often played playground ball. Later, the two attended the University of Massachusetts together. The friend called himself "The Professor" because he thought he could take opponents to school, and called Erving "The Doctor" because he could really operate. "The Doctor" quickly became "Dr. J" and often was shortened simply to "Doc" during Erving's Hall of Fame career.

Clyde: Walt Frazier was the essence of style and cool in the 1970s and liked to dress in stylish clothes that included wide-brimmed hats. One day during a road trip he bought a new hat and wore it to the game that night. When he entered the dressing room, longtime Knicks trainer Danny Whelan took one look and called him "Clyde," because it was the kind of hat worn by bank robber Clyde Barrow, who was portrayed by Warren Beatty in the popular 1967 film *Bonnie and Clyde*.

Walt Frazier did not earn his nickname by making fancy passes like the one shown here. His stylish dress off the court is why they called him "Clyde."

Machine Gun: Travis Grant scored over 4,000 points for Kentucky State from 1969 through 1972 and got his nickname because he was always firing away.

Spud: Anthony Webb became known as "Spud" because when he was born, a cousin thought his head looked like Sputnik, the first Russian space satellite. This was shortened by the family to "Spud."

Magic: Earvin Johnson was nicknamed "Magic" by a sportswriter who covered his high school games in East Lansing, Michigan. After one game, he approached the teenager and told him, "You're so good and your game is so flashy, you need a nickname." They rejected Dr. J, since that belonged to Julius Erving, and the Big E, which belonged to Elvin Hayes. Finally, the writer decided to call him "Magic," because of the way he handled the ball. The nickname fit and stuck with him throughout his career, although Johnson often has said he felt that he had two personalities: the smiling, bubbly "Magic" that fans saw on the court and in public, and a quieter, more introspective "Earvin", which he was the rest of the time. To his teammates on the Lakers, Johnson was known as "Buck" or "E.J." or Earvin, but rarely "Magic."

Movies were often the source for nicknames in the 1950s and 1960s. **John Havlicek** resembled a character in the movie *Hondo*, starring actor John Wayne.

Ack Ack: Tommy Heinsohn, a prolific scorer with the Boston Celtics in the 1950s and 1960s and later the team's coach and broadcaster, got this nickname because he liked to shoot at every opportunity and "Ack Ack" is the sound a machine gun makes.

Hondo: John Havlicek got this nickname while he was at Ohio State from teammate Mel Nowell. Havlicek liked reading Western novels and bore a resemblance to a young John Wayne, who starred in a movie called *Hondo* that was popular at the time.

The Big O: Oscar Robertson was one of the most complete basketball players ever and the only one to average a triple-double for an entire NBA season, which he did in 1961–62. At the University of Cincinnati, he led the nation in scoring three years in a row. At the same time, a James Thurber story, "The Disappearing O," about a vowel that kept disappearing, was very popular. So Robertson became "The Big O."

John Wooden is best-known for his coaching achievements at UCLA. During his playing career he was known as the "India Rubber Man."

Captain Late: James Silas, who starred for the San Antonio Spurs, was one of the top guards of the ABA. He was especially effective in clutch time, at the ends of close games, so his teammates tabbed him "Captain Late."

Sweetwater: Nat Clifton got his nickname while in high school because he liked soda so much. He played for the Harlem Globetrotters and later the New York Knicks, becoming in 1950 the first African-American to sign with an NBA team.

Pitchin' Paul: Paul Arizin scored 85 points in one game for Villanova and went on to average 22.8 points per game in a fine NBA career. He got his nickname because he was always in there pitchin', tossing up shots.

India Rubber Man: John Wooden is best known as the "Wizard of Westwood" for his brilliant coaching career at UCLA, which is located in the Westwood section of Los Angeles. But he was also an outstanding high school, college, and pro player before that in his home state of Indiana. As a three-time All-American at Purdue University, he got the nickname "India Rubber Man" because he always seemed to be bouncing up off the floor after scrambling after loose balls.

Answers to matching quiz: Greg "Cadillac" Anderson, Ken "The Animal" Bannister, Jerry "Hound" Baskerville, Nat "Sweetwater" Clifton, Artis "A Train" Gilmore, John "Hondo" Havlicek, Darrell "Dr. Dunkenstein" Griffith, Darnell "Dr. Dunk" Hillman, Gus "Honeycomb" Johnson, Bob "Butterbean" Love, Cedric "Cornbread" Maxwell, Earl "The Pearl" Monroe, Oscar "The Big O" Robertson, Glenn "Big Dog" Robinson, Dennis "Worm" Rodman, Wayne "Tree" Rollins, Bobby "Bingo" Smith, Jamaal "Silk" Wilkes, Bill "Poodles" Willoughby.

The Rifleman Breaks Glass

The first backboard to be broken in NBA history was by Chuck Connors, who went on to star in a popular 1950s TV western, *The Rifleman*. The 6' 7" Connors was an outstanding athlete who played two years of major league baseball and three seasons of professional basketball, 1945–46 with the Rochester Royals of the NBL and 1946–47 and 1947–48 with the Boston Celtics of the NBA, before launching his acting career.

He etched his name in NBA history while the Celtics and Chicago Stags teams were warming up at Boston Arena before the Celtics' first-ever game in 1946. Connors went in for a layup, grabbed the rim and the glass backboard shattered into hundreds of pieces. The start of the game was delayed while another backboard was brought crosstown from Boston Garden.

SUPER STREAKS AND FANTASTIC FINISHES

8

Basketball has seen many memorable moments over the years.

There have been some amazing streaks at all levels of competition, and the games that broke those streaks often are remembered as vividly as the streaks themselves. Buzzer-beating baskets make for memorable moments, as do clutch steals and other great plays.

Here is a look at some of basketball's greatest streaks and how they came to an end, as well as some other memorable moments from over 100 years of hoops history:

UCLA'S 88-GAME WINNING STREAK

Winning streaks were a matter of course for the UCLA Bruins under coach John Wooden. UCLA dominated college basketball from 1963 through 1974, winning seven NCAA championships in a row and 10 in 12 years. Four times during that span UCLA went undefeated. It is a period of success unmatched in college basketball history.

UCLA was riding a 47-game winning streak before Austin Carr's 46 points led Notre Dame to an 89-82 victory on January 26, 1971. That left the Bruins short of the collegiate record of 60 consecutive victories set by the University of San Francisco in the 1950s, a team that featured Hall of Famers Bill Russell and K.C. Jones.

UCLA 88-Game Win Streak

UCLA's 88-game win streak included national titles in 1971, 1972, and 1973. The streak was ended by Notre Dame in 1974.

So UCLA went out and started another winning streak, and this time San Francisco's record would fall. What's more, it would be Notre Dame that would provide UCLA with victim number 61 two years later. On January 28, 1973, UCLA defeated Notre Dame 82-63 as 6' 11" center Bill Walton scored 16 points, grabbed 15 rebounds, and blocked 10 shots. UCLA led all the way in its record-breaking game, with Walton and Larry Farmer getting 12 points apiece as the Bruins built a 38-25 halftime lead. UCLA stretched the margin to 61-39 midway through the second half and coasted home.

The record winning streak continued for another year, until UCLA met up with Notre Dame once again. They were the two top-ranked teams in the country when they collided on January 19, 1974, with the streak up to 88 consecutive wins.

With Walton hitting 12-of-13 shots, UCLA led 70-59 with 3:32 left to play when it went into a stall. The idea was to kill the clock, but instead it killed the streak. Notre Dame went into a full-court press that forced a series of UCLA turnovers. Two baskets by John Shumate and one each by Adrian Dantley and Gary Brokaw made it 70-67. Brokaw, the game's leading scorer with 25 points, capitalized on another turnover to bring Notre Dame within one with 1:11 to play.

Yet another UCLA turnover gave the Irish the ball once again, and guard Dwight Clay got free in the right corner for a long jumper. His basket with 29 seconds left put Notre Dame in front. After missed shots by Walton and Tommy Curtis and missed tips by David Meyers and Pete Trgovich, UCLA's streak had been broken.

N.C. STATE ENDS UCLA'S TITLE STREAK

No team ever has dominated college basketball the way UCLA did in the late 1960s and early 1970s, when the Bruins became the Boston Celtics of the college game. The Celtics won eight consecutive NBA titles and 11 in 13 years; UCLA's numbers would be seven in a row and 10 in 12 seasons. UCLA's reign from 1966–67 through 1972–73 is by far the longest in NCAA history—no other team has won more than two consecutive championships.

After winning seven titles in a row under coach John Wooden, UCLA looked like it would win an eighth in 1974 with a team known as the Walton Gang, built around 6' 11" senior Bill Walton. Walton was a complete center, an unusual player who could beat you with his scoring, rebounding, and passing. Other stars on that team included forwards Jamaal Wilkes and Dave Meyers.

Though UCLA's 88-game winning streak had been broken by Notre Dame in midseason, the Bruins had won their eighth straight Pacific 8 Conference title and went into the NCAA tournament eager to regain the Number 1 national ranking from North Carolina State and extend their string of championships. The Wolfpack had climbed into the top spot after losing just one game all year—but that had been to UCLA by a decisive 84-66 margin.

The same two teams met in the NCAA Semifinals, and the game lived up to all expectations. The teams were tied 35-35 at halftime following a 30-foot heave by Meyers, then the Bruins outscored N.C. State 14-3 to take an 11-point lead. That was where the margin stood with 10:56 to play when turnovers opened the door for the Wolfpack, who pulled ahead 63-61 on a three-point play by Thompson. UCLA tied the score at 65-65 with two minutes to go and neither team scored the rest of the way, so the game went into overtime.

Each team managed just one basket in the cautiously played overtime, so they went to a second extra period. This time

Walton and Wilkes combined for seven quick points and UCLA opened a 74-67 lead. But again turnovers proved UCLA's undoing, as Thompson led N.C. State on an 11-1 run and the Wolfpack won 80-77.

N.C. State had handed UCLA its first tournament loss in 39 games, a streak dating back to 1963. The dynasty was over—or at least interrupted, since UCLA would bounce back to win one more title in 1975. But after N.C. State beat Marquette 76-64, college basketball had something it hadn't had in eight years— a champion other than UCLA.

LAKERS WIN 33 IN A ROW

The Los Angeles Lakers were getting old as they entered the 1971–72 season. Team captain Elgin Baylor was 37 with bad knees, Wilt Chamberlain was 35, Jerry West was 33. They had just lost to the young Milwaukee Bucks in the playoffs, and they needed a shot in the arm.

It came from Bill Sharman, who had been hired as the Lakers' new coach. The former Boston Celtics guard had coached the Cleveland Pipers to the 1962 American Basketball League championship and the Utah Stars to the 1971 American Basketball Association title. When he came to the Lakers, he installed a running game on offense and persuaded Chamberlain not to worry about scoring but to focus on defense and rebounding in order to trigger the fast break.

Sharman also made two important lineup changes and one key psychological move. Figuring West would get his points no matter what, Sharman inserted Gail Goodrich into the starting lineup at shooting guard and told West to concentrate on play-making. When Baylor retired nine games into the season, Sharman moved young shooter Jim McMillian into the forward spot alongside rebounder Happy Hairston. And perhaps most importantly, he stroked Chamberlain's ego by naming him the new team captain.

Suddenly the Lakers caught fire. They beat the Baltimore Bullets 110-106 on November 5, 1971, and they didn't stop winning for more than two months.

On December 12, they beat the Atlanta Hawks 104-95 for their twenty-first consecutive victory, surpassing the NBA record of

20 set by Milwaukee the previous year. And on December 22, they beat the Bullets 127-120 to make it 27 in a row, beating the longest winning streak in all major league sports, 26 games by baseball's 1916 New York Giants.

On January 7, 1972, they extended their streak to 33 straight wins by beating the Hawks 134-90, but the streak was finally stopped by the Bucks 120-104 on January 9.

The streak raised the Lakers' record to 39-3 and they finished the season at 69-13, the best in NBA history until the 1995–96 Chicago Bulls went 72-10. In the NBA Playoffs they swept Chicago, defeated defending champion Milwaukee in six games, and beat New York in five to win the first championship since the team moved from Minneapolis in 1960.

Goodrich and West were the scoring leaders at 25.9 and 25.8 points per game, respectively, while West showed his versatility by leading the league in assists at 9.7 per game. Chamberlain topped the league in rebounding at 19.2 rebounds per game and field goal percentage at .649. The NBA didn't keep statistics on blocked shots until two years later, but don't bet Chamberlain didn't lead the league in that, too.

Jerry West averaged 9.2 assists and 25.8 points per game during the Lakers record-setting season.

"That team could beat you any way—on defense, on offense, on rebounding," said Sharman.

CHAMBERLAIN AND THE SIXERS END THE CELTICS' STREAK

Philadelphia almost ended Boston's streak of championships in 1965 but was thwarted by John Havlicek's famous playoff steal. The next year Philadelphia edged Boston by one game in the regular season, but lost to the Celtics in the playoffs. But 1967 was different.

The 76ers had assembled what many consider the greatest team in NBA history. The unstoppable Chamberlain, at the peak of his game, was the centerpiece. Chet Walker and Luke Jackson were forerunners of the modern pro forwards, Walker the smooth-shooting small forward, Jackson the muscular power forward. Wali Jones was a playmaker, and Hal Greer was a Hall of Fame shooting guard. The bench was led by second-year forward Billy Cunningham, another future Hall of Famer, while Larry Costello, Matt Guokas, and Billy Melchionni provided backcourt depth.

"We had everything," said Greer "We knew we were going to win most of our games—it was just a matter of by how much. It was a beautiful, beautiful season."

The Sixers went 68-13 in the regular season, at the time the best record in league history. But the Sixers knew it would mean little if they didn't beat Boston in the playoffs.

Philadelphia opened the Boston series by winning at home as expected, then stunning the Celtics in Boston 107-102. Bill Russell, the Celtics' player-coach, juggled his lineup for the third game, inserting John Havlicek and Larry Siegfried as starters, but Boston still lost, 115-104, as Chamberlain set a playoff record with 41 rebounds.

Although the Celtics saved face by winning Game 4 in Boston, it only delayed the inevitable. Philadelphia brought a decisive end to Boston's string of eight consecutive championships with a 140-116 victory in Game 5 at Convention Hall. Two weeks later, following a six-game NBA Finals against the Golden State Warriors, the Sixers were NBA champions.

"The best team I ever saw," said Chamberlain, "was the 1966–67 Philadelphia 76ers."

PAXSON IS ON TARGET FOR CHICAGO

After winning consecutive championships, Michael Jordan and the Chicago Bulls knew that if they won again in 1992–93, they would take their place in history. Only two teams in NBA history had won as many as three titles in a row, the Minneapolis Lakers in 1952–54 and the Boston Celtics in 1959–66.

"My goal was to win three straight because it was something that Isiah [Thomas] never did, something Magic [Johnson] and [Larry] Bird never did," said Jordan, referring to the teams that had preceded the Bulls atop the NBA—Thomas' Detroit Pistons, Johnson's Los Angeles Lakers, and Bird's Boston Celtics.

The third championship was not going to be easy. The Bulls won 57 games during the regular season, but Phoenix won 62 and New York 60. However, the Bulls were focused on the playoffs, where they swept Atlanta and Cleveland and beat the Knicks in six games to earn a trip to the NBA Finals against the Suns, who had added Charles Barkley in the offseason. Barkley had enjoyed his finest season and beaten out Jordan for league MVP honors.

Chicago surprised the Suns by winning the first two games in Phoenix, but the Suns took two of three in Chicago to send the series back to Phoenix, where Game 6 turned out to be a classic.

The Bulls led 87-79 going into the fourth quarter but went more than six minutes without scoring as Phoenix pulled in front. The Suns led 98-94 with 2:23 left, and suddenly the Bulls' bid to three-peat was very much in jeopardy as it looked like the series would go to a Game 7 with momentum and the home-court advantage in Phoenix's favor. But Jordan went coast-to-coast for a basket with 38.1 seconds left and Chicago regained possession after a Phoenix 24-second violation.

With 14.1 seconds left everyone expected Jordan to take the last shot. But after the ball passed through the hands of all five Chicago players, it was the Bulls' other guard, John Paxson, who found himself with an open shot from behind the three-point arc. His shot hit nothing but net with 3.9 seconds left, giving the Bulls a 99-98 victory and their third straight title.

"I just caught the ball and shot it—as I have my whole life. I've been playing basketball since I was eight years old, and I've shot like that in my driveway hundreds of thousands of times," said Paxson.

"I just had to watch and smile," said Suns Coach Paul Westphal, a former star player. "It's a shot every kid dreams about. John Paxson got to live that dream out."

THE OLYMPIC GAME WITH THREE ENDINGS

The United States had never lost in Olympic basketball, from the time the sport was introduced to medal competition in 1936 through 1968. And in 1972, with a team comprised entirely of college players, the United States won its first eight games of the tournament to move into the finals against a strong, well-coached team from the Soviet Union.

From the beginning of that gold medal game, there was a sense that the Americans might be in trouble. The Soviet Union team, much older and more experienced, slowed down the tempo, frustrating the faster, more athletic United States squad. The game came down to the final seconds when, with the Soviet Union leading by one point, Doug Collins of the United States was knocked to the floor while driving to the basket with three seconds remaining. Collins got up and sank both free throws to put the United States ahead 50-49.

Fans ran onto the court as the Soviets inbounded and play was stopped. When it was resumed, the Soviets threw the ball off the backboard and the United States recovered. The buzzer sounded and the Americans celebrated their victory.

But the Soviet coach had asked for a timeout before play resumed, a timeout that the referees had never granted. An official from the International Basketball Federation brought both teams back onto the court to replay the last three seconds. This time the Soviets got a shot off that missed, and again the Americans celebrated.

And again it was too soon. Someone noticed that 50 seconds had been put on the clock for the replay, instead of three seconds. So officials ordered that the ending of the game be played for a third time.

This time, Ivan Edeshko threw a court-length inbounds pass to Alexander Belov, standing near the foul line. Belov bumped into an American player, recovered his balance, caught the pass and got off a shot that went in at the buzzer, giving the Soviets a 51-50 victory.

The Americans were stunned at their first-ever Olympic defeat and furious at the way the ending had been replayed. United States officials formally protested, but to no avail. The team voted not to accept its silver medals in a further protest.

"I see it today as clearly as if on a videotape replay," recalled Collins. "After being so happy about the two free throws I had made, I was the most dejected person in the world. The one thing I regret, more than anything else, is not having that feeling you get standing on the platform, getting the gold medal around your neck and listening to the national anthem. I feel we were robbed of that."

The Americans suffered their first-ever Olympic baskebtall defeat at the hands of the Soviet Union team in 1972.

PHI SLAMMA JAMMA GETS DUNKED

N.C. State's **Lorenzo Charles** slams home the game-winner in the 1983 NCAA basketball final, ending the University of Houston's dream season.

They were the fraternity of dunk—the University of Houston Cougars of the early 1980s, featuring high-flying stars like Hakeem Olajuwon, Clyde Drexler, Larry Micheaux, and Benny Anders. The Cougars entered the 1983 NCAA Tournament with a 25-game winning streak and a reputation for running the floor like an NBA team and playing the game above the rim.

Houston beat Louisville (which had won the NCAA title three years earlier with a team known as the "Doctors of Dunk") 94-81 in the national semifinals and was not expected to have much trouble with finals opponent North Carolina State, which already had lost lost 10 games.

Jim Valvano, the coach of the Wolfpack, watched Houston's win over Louisville and came away impressed. "I've never seen anything like that in sixteen years of coaching college basketball," he said. "We'll try to handle their team by playing, shall I say, a slower tempo. If we get the opening tip, we may not take a shot until Tuesday morning."

The strategy worked. The Wolfpack packed their zone defense around the basket, shut down Houston's fast break and relied on its veteran backcourt of Dereck Whittenburg and

Sidney Lowe to control the pace. Houston went nearly 15 minutes before its first dunk and trailed 33-25 at the half.

Though Drexler was on the bench with foul trouble, Houston went on a 17-2 tear to start the second half, taking a 42-35 lead with 10 minutes left. But then Houston coach Guy Lewis ordered his team to stop running and go into a more patterned offense to try and run out the clock. Instead, it opened the door for North Carolina State.

With the game at a slower pace, Houston managed just four baskets the rest of the way while the Wolfpack pecked away at the lead and drew even with 1:59 to play. And after Houston freshman Alvin Franklin missed the front end of a one-and-one, N.C. State held the ball to set up one last shot.

The plan was to free Whittenburg for a jumper, but Drexler tipped the pass away. Whittenburg grabbed the ball on the bounce but was left with a desperation heave from about 30 feet away. His shot was short, but Lorenzo Charles, a 6' 7" sophomore for N.C. State, caught it on the fly and dunked with one second remaining. The crowd was stunned. N.C. State had pulled off the upset, 54-52.

Valvano, his players, and the Wolfpack fans went wild, racing about the court in celebration of the stunning upset. It was a dunk that had beaten the men of Phi Slamma Jamma, the fraternity of dunk.

LAST-SECOND LAETTNER

It was fitting that one of the great games in college basketball history should have a great ending. Defending champion Duke met a powerful Kentucky team in the East Regional Final of the 1992 NCAA Tournament. The high-scoring game had just about everything, with great players making great plays time and again. It went to overtime, and with 2.1 seconds left, 6' 2" guard Sean Woods of Kentucky flipped in a short shot over the outstretched arm of Duke's 6' 11" All-American Christian Laettner to give the Wildcats a 103-102 lead. Duke called a timeout.

"First of all, we're going to win, okay?" Duke Coach Mike Krzyzewski told his players. But 2.1 seconds isn't much time, especially when you must take the ball the length of the court and score against one of the best teams in the country.

Believe it or not, Duke had a play for just such a situation, and had even used it once in the regular season. On the play, versatile Grant Hill takes the ball out of bounds and throws a long, baseball pass to Laettner, who catches it at the opposite foul line, spins and shoots. Unfortunately, when Duke tried it in the regular season, Hill's pass sailed off to the side and Laettner came down out of bounds once he caught it. As the Duke players broke the huddle and went back onto the court following the timeout, Laettner turned to Hill and said, "I'm not going to step out this time."

As Hill prepared to throw the ball inbounds, Laettner lined up at the far foul line where he was guarded by two shorter Kentucky players—the Wildcats had lost two 6' 8" frontcourtmen, Jamal Mashburn and Gimel Martinez, on fouls. Hill's pass sailed some 70 feet, and this time it was right on target. Laettner caught it and knew he had just a little time to work with, so he made the most of it. He made a fake to his left and took one dribble to his right, then stopped and spun back to his left to shoot.

Coach Mike Krzyzewski embraces **Christian Laettner** after his last-second basket gave Duke a thrilling overtime victory in the 1992 East Regional final of the NCAA basketball tournament.

Once the shot left Laettner's hands, Krzyzewski didn't even have to watch to know it would find nothing but net, giving

Duke a 104-103 victory. "I've seen Christian shoot so much that when I saw the arc, I knew it was in," he explained.

Laettner's basket completed a magical game in which he scored 30 points on 10-for-10 from the field and 10-for-10 from the foul line. The Blue Devils went on to beat Indiana and Michigan to win their second straight NCAA Championship.

JORDAN AND WORTHY
TEAM UP FOR A TITLE

Perhaps the first time the world took notice of Michael Jordan was on March 29, 1982, when he was barely 19 years old, a freshman at the University of North Carolina. Jordan would go on to hit many big shots in his career, but the one he sank that night thrust him into the spotlight because it happened before 61,612 fans at the Louisiana Superdome in the NCAA Championship game against Georgetown.

North Carolina was ranked Number 1, largely because of its 6' 9" frontcourt stars, James Worthy and Sam Perkins. Jordan had averaged 13.5 points per game as a freshman. Opposing the Tar Heels was a Georgetown team that featured another freshman, 7' Patrick Ewing, as well as an All-American guard, Eric "Sleepy" Floyd. The game also paired two coaching legends, Dean Smith of North Carolina and John Thompson of Georgetown.

Ewing was called for several goaltending calls in the opening minutes and a total of five in the first half, but Thompson didn't mind. It was all part of Georgetown's strategy. "We wanted them to be conscious of Patrick." he said, "And if a few goaltending calls were the price that had to be paid, so be it."

The Hoyas led 32-31 at halftime and the game stayed close throughout the second half, with neither team ever pulling more than four points in front. Floyd scored with 57 seconds left to give Georgetown a 62-61 lead and then North Carolina ran some time off the clock before calling a timeout to set up a final play.

The logical choice was Worthy, a junior and a consensus All-American, but instead Smith drew it up for Jordan. The freshman worked his way free on the left side of the court, caught the ball and shot a 16-foot jumper that sailed through with 15 seconds left and put North Carolina up by one.

"I was all kinds of nervous," Jordan said of his big shot, "but I didn't have time to think about doubts. I had a feeling it was going to go in."

Georgetown still had time for one last play. Sophomore Fred Brown dribbled the ball upcourt and looked to Floyd, who was covered on the left baseline. Then he looked at the big men, but saw that Ewing and Ed Spriggs were closely guarded. He figured Eric Smith might be open on the right side. "I thought I saw Smitty out of the right corner of my eye," Brown said. "My peripheral vision is pretty good. But this time it failed me. It was only a split-second, but that's all it takes to lose a game."

The player he saw was not Smith but Worthy, who was stunned when Brown's pass came right to him. He caught it with five seconds left and was fouled three seconds later. It didn't matter that Worthy missed both free throws, because Georgetown only had time for a desperation heave that missed.

THE GENIUS OF LARRY BIRD

Red Auerbach, the longtime coach and front office executive of the Boston Celtics, used to say that what set Larry Bird apart from other players is that while others might see what was happening on the court, Bird had the basketball instincts to see things before they happened and the skill to change the result.

Bird did just that in the closing seconds of Game 5 of the 1987 Eastern Conference Finals between the Celtics and the Detroit Pistons.

Detroit led 107-106 and had possession of the ball, out of bounds in the Boston frontcourt. The Pistons needed only to run out the final five seconds to head home with a 3-2 series lead and a chance to close out the Celtics. It seemed like the young, rising Pistons were about to replace the aging Celtics as the power in the Eastern Conference.

Bird had other ideas. "When there's time left," he said, "there's always a chance."

Detroit captain Isiah Thomas prepared to toss the ball inbounds from the sideline. Bird saw Thomas glance at Pistons center Bill Laimbeer in the low post just before releasing the ball, so he cut in front and picked the ball off before it reached Laimbeer's hands. He then stopped and turned toward the foul lane, where teammate Dennis Johnson was cutting toward the basket. Bird fired a crisp pass to Johnson, who laid it in with one second remaining for a 108-107 Boston victory.

The Celtics went on to win the series in seven games to advance to the NBA Finals and a matchup with the Los Angeles Lakers. The rivals had split their two previous meetings, Boston winning the 1984 NBA Finals and the Lakers turning the tables in 1985. And though the Lakers would win the series in six games, Bird's steal against the Pistons had given the Celtics one last shot at the title. Detroit would beat Boston in six games in the 1988 Conference Finals, and the Celtics haven't gotten that far since.

MAGIC JOHNSON'S JUNIOR SKY-HOOK BEATS BOSTON

The 1987 NBA Finals was the rubber match, the third show-down between Larry Bird's Boston Celtics and Magic Johnson's Los Angeles Lakers. The Celtics had won in 1984 and the Lakers in 1985, but their next meeting was delayed a year because Houston upset Los Angeles en route to the 1986 Finals, won by Boston.

The Lakers won two of the first three games, but the Celtics grabbed a 16-point halftime lead in Game 4 in Boston Garden and looked on their way toward tying the best-of-7 series. But the Lakers fought back and chipped away at the lead, drawing within eight points with three minutes to go and within one, at 103-102, with 30 seconds left.

Johnson and Kareem Abdul-Jabbar worked the pick-and-roll to perfection to put Los Angeles in front by one, but Bird sank a three-pointer with 12 seconds left and Boston was back on top 106-104. On the next possession Abdul-Jabbar was fouled. He made the first free throw but missed the second that would have tied the score. However, the ball squirted out of bounds

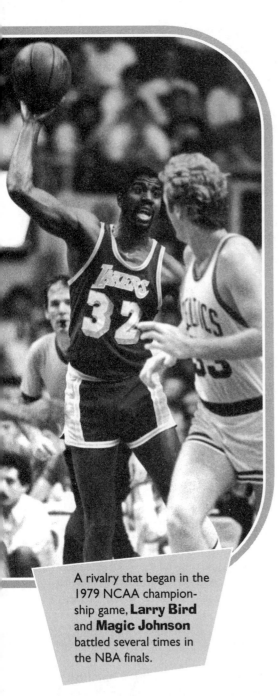

A rivalry that began in the 1979 NCAA championship game, **Larry Bird** and **Magic Johnson** battled several times in the NBA finals.

off Boston's Kevin McHale, giving the Lakers possession once again. They called a timeout to set up a play.

Johnson took the inbounds pass on the left side and at first thought about shooting a jumper, but the 6' 11" McHale leaped out at him and forced him to change his plan. So Johnson dribbled toward the key, where Bird and Robert Parish joined McHale in pursuit. Just before he reached the foul line Johnson tossed up an old-fashioned running hook shot that sailed through the net and put the Lakers in front 107-106. After Bird missed a last-second jumper, the Lakers ran off the court with a commanding 3-1 series lead, and would go on to win the series in six games.

After hitting his game-winning shot, Johnson paid homage to Abdul-Jabbar, the Lakers' center and the NBA's all-time leading scorer. Johnson called the shot "my junior, junior sky-hook," a tribute to Abdul-Jabbar's favorite shot.

Bird just shook his head and smiled. "You expect to lose to the Lakers on a sky-hook," he said. "You don't expect it to be from Magic."

THE GREATEST GAME EVER PLAYED?

There have been so many great games in basketball history, it's hard to label one as "the greatest." But for anyone who was at Boston Garden on Friday night, June 4, 1976, there really is no debate.

Game 5 of the 1976 NBA Finals between the Phoenix Suns and Boston Celtics had everything—a great setting, outstanding plays, brilliant strategy, clutch baskets, surprise heroes, and more than its share of controversy. It even had three overtime periods, for those who can't get enough of a good thing!

The more experienced Celtics were highly favored to win the championship over the Suns, but the teams split the first four games, each winning twice on its home court. Boston hoped to continue the pattern in Game 5 and jumped out to a 61-45 half-time advantage, and with 3:49 to play, the Celtics still led by nine.

In the next three minutes, however, Suns guard Paul Westphal, a former Celtic, scored nine of his team's next 11 points, and the game was tied with 39 seconds to play. Curtis Perry hit a free throw for Phoenix and 36-year-old John Havlicek, playing despite a broken bone in his foot, hit one for Boston to send the game into overtime tied 95-95.

Two late baskets by Perry overcame a four-point Boston lead and forced a second overtime period, but not before the first of several controversies arose. The Suns argued that Paul Silas had requested a timeout in the closing seconds, and since Boston did not have any timeouts left, a technical foul should have been called, giving Phoenix a chance to win the game. But referee Richie Powers either didn't see or didn't grant Silas's request and the final buzzer sounded, infuriating the Suns' bench.

In the second overtime, Boston led 109-106 with 39 seconds left but a basket by Dick Van Arsdale was followed by a Westphal steal and Perry basket for a 110-109 Phoenix lead. With five seconds left, Havlicek took the inbounds pass, drove toward the hoop and put up a running one-hander that went in with one second left. Fans poured onto the court and the clock went down to zero, even though Phoenix had not put the ball back in play. Amidst the chaos, Powers stood under the basket blowing his whistle and waving his arms, signaling that the game was not yet over.

It took 10 minutes for order to be restored, during which time one fan had punched Powers and others had gotten involved in a tussle with the Phoenix players. But finally, one second was put back on the clock and Phoenix given the ball.

During the delay, Westphal suggested to Coach John MacLeod that the Suns do what Silas had done—request a timeout the team didn't have. They would make sure the referees gave them a technical foul, which would give Boston a free throw and the chance to raise the lead to two points. But after the timeout, Phoenix would get to inbound the ball from midcourt instead of from under its own basket and thus be in better position for a last-second shot.

The strategy worked. Jo Jo White made the free throw following the technical foul, but Phoenix's inbounds pass from midcourt was easily caught by Heard at the top of the key. He turned and shot and his jumper went through at the buzzer, forcing a third overtime.

By now everyone was drained—players, coaches, and fans. Several players from both teams had fouled out, but it was the Celtics who came up with the unlikely hero. Glenn McDonald, a little-used rookie who would have a brief and otherwise obscure pro career, scored six of Boston's 12 points in the third overtime and the Celtics came away with a 128-126 victory.

"That was the most exciting basketball game I've ever seen," said Hall of Famer Rick Barry, who broadcast the game. "They just had one great play after another. It was such an emotional and physical game for everybody involved."

Two days later in Phoenix, Boston closed out the series with an 87-80 win, giving the Celtics the 1976 NBA championship.

Buzzer-Beaters

Throughout his luminous NBA career, Michael Jordan has tormented every one of his opponents on the court. Whether it was with a space-shuttle slam, a dominant scoring stretch that assured a Chicago Bulls victory, or a game-long assault that filled the highlight reels, it wasn't long before Jordan's rivals were reduced to mere spectators.

Every team in the league has had its special "Air Jordan" nightmare, but the Cleveland Cavaliers are perhaps the most haunted. Twice Jordan nailed jump shots at the buzzer to win a playoff series over the Cavs—both times in Cleveland's Richfield Coliseum. The game-winning lightning bolts might have been mere journal entries in Jordan's amazing personal record, but they were devastating to Cleveland, which had spent the latter years of Jordan's career in a futile attempt to supplant the Bulls at the top of the Eastern Conference. Jordan's first buzzer-beater was the most costly, coming in the fifth and deciding game of a 1989 first-round playoff series. With the Cavaliers clinging to a 100-99 lead, Jordan pulled up just to the left of the key and drilled a jump shot over Craig Ehlo as time expired. The footage of Jordan leaping in the air to celebrate while Ehlo and his Cleveland teammates slumped to the ground in defeat has been replayed over and over again.

Jordan's second fatal blow to Cleveland's playoff hopes wasn't quite as dramatic. It merely served as an exclamation point to the Bulls' four-game sweep of the Cavs in the 1993 Eastern Conference Semifinals. With Game 4 tied at 101 apiece and time running out, Jordan rose over Gerald Wilkins and dropped in the game-winning shot.

As great as he is, Michael Jordan certainly isn't the first NBA player to win or tie a crucial game with a thrilling, last-second shot. Buzzer-beaters are as old as the league itself and have helped cement the legends of some teams and players while derailing the hopes and dreams of others.

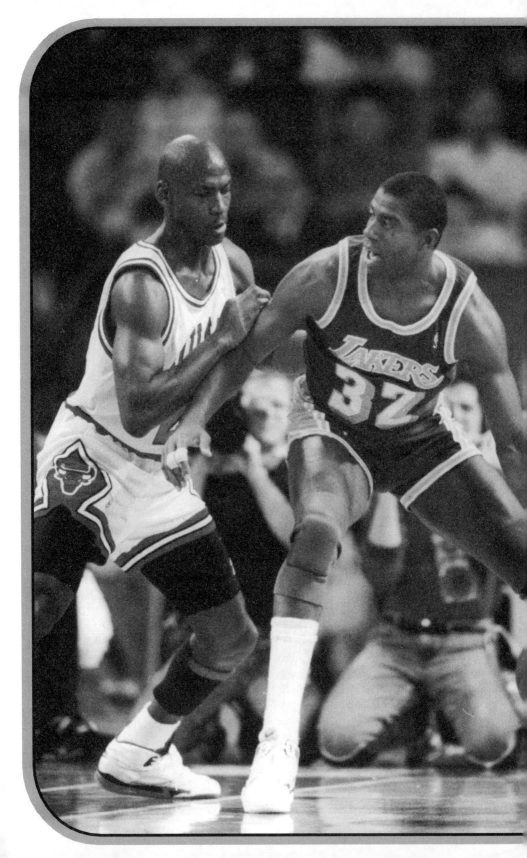

APPENDIX

MEMBERS OF THE NAISMITH MEMORIAL BASKETBALL HALL OF FAME

There have been 222 individuals and four teams elected to the Naismith Memorial Basketball Hall of Fame in Springfield, Massachusetts, the shrine that honors people from all segments of the sport. The seven most recent electees, enshrined on September 29, 1997, are former NBA stars Alex English and Bailey Howell, coaches Pete Carril, Don Haskins and Antonio Diaz-Miguel and women's basketball stars Denise Curry and Joan Crawford.

THE COMPLETE LIST OF ELECTEES TO THE BASKETBALL HALL OF FAME

Contributors

Name	Year Elected	Name	Year Elected
Senda Berenson Abbott	1984	Ferenc Hepp	1980
Clair Bee	1967	Edward J. Hickcox	1959
Walter A. Brown	1965	Paul D. (Tony) Hinkle	1965
John W. Bunn	1964	Edward S. (Ned) Irish	1964
Robert L. Douglas	1971	R. William Jones	1964
Alva O. Duer	1981	J. Walter Kennedy	1980
Clifford B. Fagan	1983	Emil S. Liston	1974
Harry A. Fisher	1973	William G. Mokray	1965
Lawrence Fleisher	1991	Ralph Morgan	1959
Edward Gottlieb	1971	Frank Morganweck	1962
Luther H. Gulick	1959	James Naismith	1959
Lester Harrison	1979	John J. O'Brien	1961

Contributors (continued)

Name	Year Elected	Name	Year Elected
Lawrence F. O'Brien	1991	Amos Alonzo Stagg	1959
Harold G. Olsen	1959	Borislav Stankovic	1991
Maurice Podoloff	1973	Edward S. Steitz	1983
Henry V. Porter	1960	Charles H. (Chuck) Taylor	1968
William A. Reid	1963	Bertha F. Teague	1984
Elmer H. Ripley	1972	Osward Tower	1959
Lynn W. St. John	1962	Arthur L. Trester	1961
Abraham Saperstein	1970	W.R. Clifford Wells	1971
Arthur A. Schabinger	1961	Louis G. Wilke	1982

Players

Name	Year Elected	Name	Year Elected
Kareem Abdul-Jabbar	1995	Robert E. Davies	1969
Nathaniel (Nate) Archibald	1991	Forrest S. DeBernardi	1961
Paul J. Arizin	1977	David A. DeBusschere	1982
Thomas B. Barlow	1980	Henry G. (Dutch) Dehnert	1968
Richard F. (Rick) Barry	1987	Anne Donovan	1995
Elgin Baylor	1976	Paul Endacott	1971
John Beckman	1972	Alex English	1997
Walt Bellamy	1993	Julius W. Erving	1993
Sergei Belov	1992	Harold E. (Bud) Foster	1964
Dave Bing	1990	Walter Frazier	1987
Carol Blazejowski	1994	Max (Marty) Friedman	1971
Bernard (Bennie) Borgmann	1961	Joseph F. Fulks	1977
William W. Bradley	1982	Lauren (Laddie) Gale	1976
Joseph R. Brennan	1974	Harry J. Gallatin	1991
Alfred N. Cervi	1984	William (Pop) Gates	1989
Wilton N. Chamberlain	1978	George Gervin	1996
Charles T. (Tarzan) Cooper	1976	Thomas J. Gola	1975
Kresimir Cosic	1996	Gail Goodrich	1996
Robert J. Cousy	1970	Harold E. (Hal) Greer	1981
David W. Cowens	1991	Robert F. (Ace) Gruenig	1963
Joan Crawford	1997	Clifford O. Hagan	1977
William J. Cunningham	1985	Victor A. Hanson	1960
Denise Curry	1997	Lusia Harris	1992
		John Havlicek	1983
		Connie Hawkins	1992
		Elvin E. Hayes	1990

Players (continued)

Name	Year Elected	Name	Year Elected
Thomas W. Heinsohn	1985	Charles C. (Stretch) Murphy	1960
Nat Holman	1964	Harlon O. (Pat) Page	1962
Robert J. Houbregs	1987	Robert L. Pettit	1970
Bailey Howell	1997	Andy Phillip	1961
Charles D. (Chuck) Hyatt	1959	James C. Pollard	1977
Dan P. Issel	1993	Frank V. Ramsey	1981
Harry (Buddy) Jennette	1994	Willis Reed	1981
William C. Johnson	1976	Oscar P. Robertson	1979
Donald Neil Johnston	1990	John S. Roosma	1961
K.C. Jones	1989	John D. (Honey) Russell	1964
Samuel Jones	1983	William F. Russell	1974
Edward W. (Moose) Krause	1975	Adolph Schayes	1972
Robert A. Kurland	1961	Ernest J. Schmidt	1973
Robert J. Lanier	1992	John J. Schommer	1959
Joe Lapchick	1966	Barney Sedran	1962
Nancy Lieberman-Cline	1996	Uljana Semjonova	1993
Clyde E. Lovellette	1988	William W. Sharman	1975
Jerry R. Lucas	1979	Christian Steinmetz	1961
Angelo (Hank) Luisetti	1959	David Thompson	1996
Branch McCracken	1960	John A. Thompson	1962
Jack McCracken	1962	Nate Thurmond	1984
Robert McDermott	1988	John K. Twyman	1982
Edward C. Macauley	1960	Westly Unseld	1988
Peter P. Maravich	1987	Robert P. (Fuzzy) Vandivier	1974
Slater N. Martin	1981	Edward A. Wachter	1961
Richard S. McGuire	1993	William T. Walton	1993
Ann E. Meyers	1993	Robert F. Wanzer	1987
George L. Mikan	1959	Jerry A. West	1979
Vern Mikkelsen	1995	Nera White	1992
Cheryl Miller	1995	Leonard R. Wilkens	1989
Earl Monroe	1990	John R. Wooden	1960
Calvin J. Murphy	1993	George Yardley	1996

Coaches

Name	Year Elected	Name	Year Elected
Forrest C. (Phog) Allen	1959	Frank W. Keaney	1960
Harold Anderson	1984	George E. Keogan	1961
Arnold J. (Red) Auerbach	1968	Robert M. Knight	1991
Justin M. (Sam) Barry	1978	John Kundla	1995
Ernest A. Blood	1960	Ward L. Lambert	1960
Howard G. Cann	1967	Harry Litwack	1975
H. Clifford Carlson	1959	Kenneth D. Loeffler	1964
Louis P. Carnesseca	1992	Arthur C. (Dutch)	
Bernard L. (Ben)		Lonborg	1972
Carnevale	1969	Arad A. McCutcheon	1980
Pete Carril	1997	Al McGuire	1992
Everett N. Case	1981	Frank J. McGuire	1976
Denny E. Crum	1994	John B. McLendon	1978
Charles J. (Chuck) Daly	1994	Walter E. Meanwell	1959
Everett S. Dean	1966	Raymond J. Meyer	1978
Antonio Diaz-Miguel	1997	Ralph H. Miller	1988
Edgar A. Diddle	1971	Peter F. Newell	1978
Bruce Drake	1972	Jack T. Ramsay	1992
Clarence E. Gaines	1981	Cesare Rubini	1994
James H. (Jack) Gardner	1983	Adolph F. Rupp	1968
Amory T. (Slats) Gill	1967	Leonard D. Sachs	1961
Aleksandr Gomelsky	1995	Everett F. Shelton	1979
Marv K. Harshman	1984	Deam E. Smith	1982
Don Haskins	1997	Fred R. Taylor	1985
Edgar S. Hickey	1978	Margaret Wade	1984
Howard A. Hobson	1965	Stanley H. Watts	1985
William (Red) Holzman	1985	John R. Wooden	1972
Henry P. (Hank) Iba	1968	Phillip D. Woolpert	1992
Alvin F. (Doggie) Julian	1967		

Referees

Name	Year Elected	Name	Year Elected
James E. Enright	1978	John P. Nucatola	1977
George T. Hepbron	1960	Ernest C. Quigley	1961
George H. Hoyt	1961	J. Dallas Shirley	1979
Matthew P. Kennedy	1959	Earl Strom	1995
Lloyd R. Leith	1982	David Tobey	1961
Zigmund J. (Red) Mihalik	1985	David H. Walsh	1961

Teams

Name	Year Elected
First Team	1959
Original Celtics	1959
Buffalo Germans	1961
Renaissance	1963

APPENDIX

BASKETBALL GLOSSARY

Airball: A shot that misses the basket and the backboard completely, hitting nothing but air.

Alley-oop: A pass that is lobbed toward the basket, where a teammate catches it and puts it in.

American Basketball Association: A professional league that existed for nine seasons, from 1967–68 through 1975–76.

American Basketball League: A name that has been used by several leagues, including a women's professional league that began play in 1996–97. Also, one of the most significant early men's professional leagues, founded in 1926 and operated off and on through the 1930s. Another ABL operated for one and a half seasons in the early 1960s.

Assist: A pass by a player that leads directly to a basket.

Backboard: The flat surface to which the basket is attached.

Backcourt: The defensive half of the court (opposite of frontcourt). Also, a team's guards are called its backcourt, or backcourtmen.

Back door play: A basic play in which the ball is passed into a pivotman and either the passer or another player fakes to the outside, then makes a sharp cut to the basket and the ball is passed to him for a layup or dunk.

Ball fake: Using the ball in order to fake a defender out of position. An offensive player might use a ball fake to fake a pass to his left to get his defender to lean in that direction, then drive to his right before the defender can recover.

Bank shot: A shot that is aimed so that it caroms off the backboard and into the basket.

Basket: A score, also known as a field goal. Also, the metal ring through which the ball must pass for a score.

Block: To deflect away a shot attempt.

Blocking: A foul in which a defensive player moves into the way of, and makes contact with, an offensive player.

Boards: Short for backboards. Also, slang for rebounds.

Bounce pass: A pass in which one offensive player advances the ball past a defender by bouncing it to a teammate.

Box out: When one player positions his body between an opposing player and the basket in order to be in prime rebounding position, he is said to be boxing out his man.

Brick: A wild shot that slams off the backboard or the rim.

CBA: The Continental Basketball Association, the sport's primary minor league.

Center: One of the three positions on a team, with guard and forward. Usually the tallest player on a team and the player who plays closest to the basket. A center is also called a pivot-man.

Center circle: The circle in the center of the court in which the opening jump ball is held.

Charging: A foul in which an offensive player runs into a defender who is stationary.

Chucker: A player who shoots frequently, sometimes too frequently. Also known as a gunner.

Coast to coast: From one end of the court to another. When a player grabs a rebound, dribbles the length of the court and scores on a layup or a dunk, he is said to have gone coast to coast.

Collective bargaining agreement: The agreement between the NBA and its Players Association that spells out players' working conditions such as salary, benefits and other conditions of employment.

Commissioner: The chief executive of the NBA, currently David J. Stern.

Court: The area on which a game is played.

Cut: A quick running move by an offensive player, usually toward the basket.

Deny the ball: Prevent an opponent from catching the ball by guarding him closely.

Dish: Pass, as in dish the ball.

Double dribble: A ballhandling violation in which a player dribbles the ball, stops, then begins to dribble again. Also, a violation in which a player dribbled the ball with both hands. The penalty is loss of possession of the ball.

Double figures: 10 or more in a statistical category. A player who scores 10 or more points is said to have scored in double figures.

Double-team: Using two defenders to guard one offensive player, thus making it harder for him to score.

Downtown: Beyond the three-point line.

Dribble: To bounce the ball in order to advance into better position.

Drive: A fast move with the ball toward the basket.

Dunk: A basket made by throwing the ball down through the hoop. Also called a slam dunk or a jam.

End line: The line at each end of the court that joins the two sidelines.

English: Spin on a ball, from the way it is released by a shooter.

Fast break: When one team attempts to score quickly by moving the ball downcourt before the other team can get in position to play defense.

FIBA: The International Basketball Federation, based in Geneva, Switzerland, the sport's global governing body.

Field goal: a basket, worth two points (or three if taken from beyond the three-point line).

Final Four: The semifinals and finals of the NCAA Basketball Championships.

Flagrant foul: In the NBA, unnecessary or excessive contact committed against an opponent.

Forward: One of three positions, with center and guard. A forward is generally a mid-sized player who plays relatively close to the basket, though not as close as the center. There are two forwards and they have become divided according to primary responsibility into power forward, or rebounder, and small forward, or scorer.

Foul: An infraction of the rules. Fouls are broken down into several categories: personal fouls are committed and charged to individual players, team fouls are the sum of all personal fouls committed by a team's players, and technical fouls are generally unsportsmanlike actions, gestures or words.

Foul circle: The circle around each foul line.

Foul line: The lines 15 feet from each basket from which free throws are attempted.

Foul shot: see free throw.

Free throw: A shot made after a foul, from the foul line (or free throw line), worth one point. Also known as a foul shot.

Frontcourt: A team's offensive half of the court. Also, a team's center and two forwards are called its frontcourt or frontcourtmen.

Full-court press: A defensive tactic in which a team's players guard their opponents closely over the entire length of the court. A variation would be a half-court press, in which a team guards its opponents closely once they cross the midcourt line.

Give-and-go: Another basic play in which a player with the ball passes it to a teammate and then breaks for the basket to take a return pass for a layup or dunk.

Glass: Slang for backboard. A good rebounder is said to be able to clean the glass.

Goaltending: A violation in which a defensive player blocks a shot while it is on the downward arc toward the basket, or a player from either team interferes with a shot while it is directly above the rim.

Guard: One of three positions, with center and forward. Usually the shortest players on a team who play furthest from the basket and pass, dribble and shoot from long range. There are two guards on a team, one known as the point guard who is primarily responsible for handling the ball and running the team's offense, and the other known as shooting guard who is primarily a scorer.

Hand-checking: Keeping a hand on a player while guarding him. Generally, if this impedes the player's progress, it is a foul.

Hardwood: Slang for the wooden floor on which games are played.

Held ball: When two players from opposing teams take possession of the ball at the same time. In the NBA this results in a jump ball, while in college teams alternate which one gets possession.

High post: A pivot position near the foul line.

Hit the open man: Find an unguarded offensive player and pass him the ball.

Hook shot: A shot in which a player, standing either with his back to the basket or sideways, extends his arm high over his head to release the ball over a defender. It can be taken while stationary, while jumping in the air (a jump-hook) or while dribbling a driving toward the basket (a running hook).

Hoop: Slang for basket.

Illegal defense: In the NBA, when a player or team violates the guidelines for playing defense which state that a player may not guard an area of the court (or play a zone) or double-team a player who does not have the ball.

In the paint: In the free-throw lane, which is painted a different color from the main color of the court.

Isolation: An offensive play in which one player is left along to maneuver against one defender, to go one-on-one.

Jump ball: In order to put the ball into play, a referee tosses the ball into the air between two players who jump and try to tap it to a teammate.

Jump shot: A shot that is attempted while jumping in the air.

Kill the clock: Use up time. A team with a lead late in a game will take as much time as possible before attempting a shot, thus giving the opposing team less time in which to try to catch up.

Lane: The area on a court, painted a different color, extending from the foul line to the end line beneath the basket. An offensive player may not stand in that area for three seconds, or a violation is called. Also called the foul lane, the free throw lane or the key (because the lane together with the foul circle originally were shaped like a keyhole).

Layup: A short shot in which a player lays the ball into the basket, usually by caroming it off the backboard.

Loose ball foul: A foul committed when neither team is in possession of the ball.

Low post: A pivot position close to the basket.

Man-to-man: A defense in which a player guards a specific opponent.

Midcourt line: The line that divided the court in half, separating the frontcourt from the backcourt.

Mismatch: When one player has a significant physical advantage over another. This is usually in height but could also be in quickness or strength. It can also be applied to one team as compared to another.

NBA: The National Basketball Association, the sport's major professional league which comprises 29 teams in the United States and Canada.

NCAA: The National Collegiate Athletic Association, which governs intercollegiate athletics.

NIT: The National Invitation Tournament, the oldest post-season collegiate tournament founded in 1938, now secondary in importance to the NCAA tournament.

Net: The cord that hangs from the basket ring.

Nothing but net: A shot that goes through the basket without touching either the rim or the backboard is said to have touched nothing but net.

One-on-one: When one offensive player maneuvers to get off his shot against one defender, without help from a teammate, he is said to be going one-on-one.

Open man: An offensive player who is unguarded.

Outlet pass: A long pass thrown after a rebound, usually to start (or trigger) a fast break.

Palming: A violation in which a player dribbling the ball moves his hand under the ball to scoop it, usually to help him change direction. Also called carrying the ball.

Penalty situation: When a team commits more than the allowed number of fouls in a period, it is said to be in the penalty situation because any future fouls result in free throws or additional free throws.

Penetration: An aggressive move toward the basket by a player dribbling the ball. Similar to a drive.

Personal foul: An infraction committed by a player that involves contact with another player, such as holding or hacking.

Pick: see Screen.

Pick-and-roll: One of the most basic plays in basketball, involving two offensive players. One sets a pick for his teammate who has the ball, then rolls or moves toward the basket or an open area of the floor. Depending on how the defense reacts, the player with the ball can either drive to the basket, take a shot or pass the ball to his teammate. Also called "screen-and-roll."

Pill: Slang for ball.

Pivot: A position taken, usually by a center, with his back to the basket.

Playmaker: A team's principal ballhandler, or point guard.

Post up: A player positions himself against a defender, with his back to the basket, is said to be posting up. He then catches a pass and spins one way or the other toward the basket for a shot.

Press: To guard an opponent closely.

Pump fake: To fake a shot in order to get a defender to jump in the air. When the defender comes down, the player with the ball can go up for an unobstructed shot.

Rebound: A missed shot that is recovered, by either the defensive or offensive team. Also the act of recovering a missed shot.

Referee: The official who conducts a game. Referees work in either two or three-man teams. One may be designated the lead official, another an umpire, or they may all be called referees; all call the same violations.

Rim: The basket ring.

Rock: Slang for ball.

Screen: When a player stands in between a teammate and the man trying to guard him, using his body as a barrier in order to given his teammate a chance to get off a shot, he is said to be setting a screen.

Set shot: A shot taken from a set position, with either one or two hands.

Shake and bake: Fancy faking by a player as he drives against a defender.

Shot clock: The clock in pro or college games that indicates how much time a team has in which to attempt a shot. If the shot clock reaches zero and the buzzer sounds, it is a violation and the defensive team gains possession of the ball.

Sky-hook: A hook shot lofted from very high, that seems to come out of the sky. This was Kareem Abdul-Jabbar's favorite shot.

Steal: Take the ball away from an opponent.

Strong side: The side of the court where the ball is. Opposite of weak side.

Switch: When two players playing man-to-man defense change the men whom they are guarding, in order to better cover their opponents during the course of a play, it is called a switch.

Technical foul: A violation, generally for unsportsmanlike actions, gestures or words. A technical foul may be called against anyone on the court or on a team's bench. A technical foul also is called after the second illegal defense violation in the NBA, or after the second delay of game violation.

Three-point line (or arc): A marking on the court, beyond which any successful shot counts for three points instead of two.

Three-sixty: To spin all the way around (360 degrees) before shooting.

Tip-in: A basket that is scored by tipping the ball into the basket, as opposed to catching it and shooting it in.

Tip-off: The jump ball that starts a game, or period of play.

Trailer: An offensive player who follows behind the ballhandler on a fast break. If the players in the first wave of the fast break are covered, the ballhandler may choose to drop the ball off to a trailer.

Transition: When a team goes from offense to defense, or vice versa.

Trap: When a second defender comes over to help the primary defender guard a man, they are said to trap or double-team him.

Traveling: A violation in which a player with the ball takes two steps without dribbling. Also called walking.

Triple-double: A player who reaches 10 or more in each of three of the five major statistical categories (points, rebounds, assists, blocks, steals) in the same game is said to have recorded a triple-double. It is a measure of all-around excellence.

Turnover: When a team loses possession of the ball without getting a shot at the basket.

USBL: The United States Basketball League, a summer professional minor league

WNBA: The Women's National Basketball Association, a summer women's professional league backed by the NBA that began competition in 1997.

Zone: A type of defense in which a player guards an area of the court, rather than a specific man.

Zone press: A more aggressive form of a zone defense, in which players guard areas of the floor, that may be applied over the full court or half court.

INDEX